Group Activities
Fired Up for Performance

Mary Keene
Loyola College in Maryland

Bradley T. Erford
Loyola College in Maryland

PEARSON

Merrill
Prentice Hall

Upper Saddle River, New Jersey
Columbus, Ohio

Library of Congress Cataloging-in-Publication Data

Keene, Mary.
  Group activities : fired up for performance / Mary Keene, Bradley T. Erford.
  p. cm.
  ISBN 0-13-170904-6
  1. Activity programs in education. 2. Educational counseling. 3. Student activities. I.
Erford, Bradley T. II. Title.

LB1027.25.K43 2007
371.4—dc22

2005058607

Vice President and Executive Publisher: Jeffery W. Johnston
Publisher: Kevin M. Davis
Editorial Assistant: Sarah N. Kenoyer
Production Editor: Mary Harlan
Design Coordinator: Diane C. Lorenzo
Illustrations: Julia Thompson
Cover Design: Candace Rowley
Cover Image: SuperStock
Production Manager: Laura Messerly
Director of Marketing: Ann Castel Davis
Marketing Manager: Autumn Purdy
Marketing Coordinator: Brian Mounts

This book was printed and bound by Bind Rite Graphics. The cover was printed by Phoenix Color Corp.

Pearson Education Ltd.
Pearson Education Singapore Pte. Ltd.
Pearson Education Canada, Ltd.
Pearson Education–Japan

Pearson Education Australia Pty. Limited
Pearson Education North Asia Ltd.
Pearson Educación de Mexico, S.A. de C.V.
Pearson Education Malaysia Pte. Ltd.

10 9 8 7 6 5 4 3 2 1
ISBN: 0-13-170904-6

Dedication

To my family for their endless patience and to all the students with whom I have spent many happy and playful hours engaging in these activities.

Mary Keene

This effort is dedicated to The One: the Giver of energy, passion, and understanding; who makes life worth living and endeavors worth pursuing and accomplishing; the Teacher of love and forgiveness.

Brad Erford

Acknowledgments

The authors would like to thank Kami McNinch and Lauren Klein for their tireless assistance in the production of this book. We are grateful for the helpful comments and suggestions of those who reviewed the manuscript: Deryl F. Bailey, University of Georgia; Robert Barret, University of North Carolina, Charlotte; Breda Bova, University of New Mexico; Tony W. Cawthon, Clemson University; and Sandy Magnuson, University of Northern Colorado.

About the Authors

Mary Keene, M.Ed., is an experienced professional school counselor and former teacher who has worked in the Baltimore County Public School System for more than 25 years. She is an affiliate faculty member in the school counseling program at Loyola College in Maryland. She is Past President of the Maryland Association for Counseling and Development (MACD), and the Maryland School Counseling Association (MSCA). Mary is an experienced and energetic workshop and leadership development facilitator.

Bradley T. Erford, Ph.D., is the Director of the School Counseling Program and an Associate Professor of Education at Loyola College in Maryland. He is the recipient of numerous awards from the American Counseling Association (ACA), Association for Counselor Education and Supervision (ACES), and Maryland Association for Counseling and Development (MACD). His research specialization falls primarily in development and technical analysis of psycho-educational tests and has resulted in the publication of four books, numerous journal articles, numerous book chapters, and eight psycho-educational tests. He is past chair of the American Counseling Association (ACA) – Southern (US) Region, past president of the Association for Assessment in Counseling and Education (AACE), and past president of the Maryland Association for Counseling and Development (MACD) and several of its divisions. Dr. Erford is a Licensed Clinical Professional Counselor, Licensed Professional Counselor, Nationally Certified Counselor, Licensed Psychologist, and Licensed School Psychologist. He teaches courses primarily in the areas of assessment, human development, school counseling, and stress management.

Fired Up for Performance:
Energizing Group Activities for Every Occasion

How to Use This Book

Have you ever wanted to make group sessions and presentations more fun and interesting? This book provides group work activities that can be easily implemented and adapted for use in small group counseling, classroom or developmental guidance, and workshops or presentations. Most activities can be used with participants from six years of age to adulthood and are appropriate for diverse groups of participants. This book is an excellent resource book for students learning to facilitate group work, group work specialists, professional counselors, and others who provide large group developmental guidance, staff development, and inservice training.

The workbook-style format provides step-by-step directions on how to implement each activity. The activities are separated according to five purposes or goals: Starters, Energizers, Communication, Team Building, and Closure. *Starters* are designed to help participants get to know each other either through dyadic, small group, or large group introductions and sharing. They are meant to get participants out of their seats and into the action. Starters are so named because they are usually used at the beginning of a session to get things going and help people meet and learn (or recall) the names of the other group members.

Energizers are also action-focused activities meant to juice up presentations or serve as "activity breaks" after a more sedentary activity. Most of the Energizers get people out of their seats and engaged in structured activities with other group members.

Communication activities get participants talking to each other in dyads or small groups about various topics requiring varying levels of disclosure. Many Communication scenarios are focused on structured activities that require participants to work together and enhance group communication to accomplish the task. Some activities rely on surface level communications, while others require deeper degrees of self-disclosure.

Team Building activities are so named because they require participants to work in small groups, communicate clearly, and develop camaraderie in order to accomplish the group task. Most of the Team Building activities feature high energy, cooperative efforts to identify and creatively solve the issues contributing to the contrived group dilemmas. These activities are designed to get the group to develop a closeness that will help them to confidently tackle future tasks with a team mentality.

Closure activities allow participants to consolidate learning, say goodbye to group mates, and attend to any unfinished business prior to the ending of the group experience. Generally these activities involve some reflection upon what has been learned or accomplished during the preceding time together and a sharing of those thoughts or insights with other participants.

Taken together, these five categories of activities can add spice to every component of a group learning experience. However, these activities are meant as stimuli for deeper learning experiences, so the skill of the facilitator and quality of learning content and instructional skills are just as important. Facilitators are encouraged to modify and adapt these activities to the audience and use the suggested variations for many of the activities. In addition, while the activities and illustrations are copyright protected, individuals who purchase this book are allowed to make copies of the illustrations for use with participants during the implementation of these activities. Many of the figures will need to be enlarged before copying.

Before we get started with these activities, let's take a look at some creative (and totally random) ways of forming teams and choosing a group leader for a given activity.

30 Creative Ways to Form Teams

Many of the activities contained in the book require the facilitator to divide participants in teams or groups. Grouping should be done in a fun way so no participant feels left out. Let your creativity be your guide. But watch out! Kids and some adults will do just about anything to get on the same team as a friend or acquaintance. In each case below, you create the number of teams you want. For instance, in the first method below, if you want eight teams, you should use eight colors. Thirty of the many ways to create teams include:

1. Colored dots.
2. Cards of different shapes.
3. Colored paper clips.
4. Pictures placed on cards to represent different types of foods, books, music, vacation sites, baseball teams, etc.
5. (Laminated) comic strip frames. (Participants who match the characters in the frames are teammates.)
6. Pictures of players from favorite teams.
7. NASCAR drivers.
8. Playing cards (by suit or number).
9. Different roles (circus, play, family, etc.).
10. Favorite holidays.
11. Cut out newspaper articles on various topics (and laminate).
12. Silhouettes of different animals, activities, etc.
13. City, county, state, or country of residence.
14. Puzzle pieces. (Put dots on the back and the first activity can be for teammates to find each other and put the puzzle together.)
15. Different feelings.
16. Favorite flavor of ice cream.
17. Zodiac signs.
18. Favorite animal or animal sound.

19. Favorite sport.

20. Favorite music group or type of music.

21. Songs.

22. Math symbols.

23. Holiday symbols.

24. Types of nuts.

25. Jobs in a company.

26. Pass out and sort by types of candy, gum, or mints.

27. Sporting equipment.

28. Cooking or table utensils.

29. Buttons with different themes.

30. Trees, flowers, plants, insects, and on and on and on...

Let your creative juices flow and, oh, the fun you'll have!!!

Choosing a Leader

When working in groups, you want activities to be fast paced and unstressful. Sometimes you may need to appoint someone to organize the group or just start things off. The following ways to select leaders are fun, random, and fair! To select group leaders, ask who:

1. Has the most buttons on their clothing.
2. Is the youngest.
3. Has the oldest pet.
4. Has the most unusual pet.
5. Has the longest lifeline on the palm of their hand.
6. Is the tallest (or shortest) group member.
7. First letter of first name is closest to the letter R.
8. Is wearing the most rings.
9. Ate the healthiest breakfast.
10. Was at a movie most recently.
11. Has the longest (shortest) hair.
12. Has worked at a job the longest.
13. Has the longest fingernails.
14. Is in the middle in height of all the group members.
15. Has taken a vacation the farthest away.
16. Drives the oldest car.
17. Plays the largest musical instrument.
18. Watched the most (least) TV the day before.
19. Has the most letters in their first (last) name.
20. Anything else you can think of; let your imagination run free!

All right everyone, let's get Fired Up!!

Contents

Section A

Starters

A1   It's Your Turn To Run for Office!

| **Goal**: Starter | **Ages**: 8-Adult | **Time**: 10 minutes |

Directions:

1. Inform participants that, at last, each will have a chance to run for office!
2. Each participant must create a slogan, poster, campaign button, song, or original speech about their positive traits.
3. After about five minutes, ask each person to present the product to the rest of the group as an introduction.

Variations:

⇒   For large groups, have participants break into groups of about 10 for the sharing portion.

| **Materials**: Paper, markers, tape, scissors | **Setup**: None | **Group Size**: Any size |

A2   The Totem Pole

| **Goal**: Starter | **Ages**: 5-Adult | **Time**: 10-15 minutes |

Directions:

1. Tell the group that a totem pole is usually a wood carving that uses animal heads and bodies to tell Native American legends. Today they have a chance to make a totem pole that will introduce their family to the group.
2. Give each table a paper bag full of materials to make a totem pole. Instruct each participant to create a totem pole that represents their family.
3. After the totem poles are finished have each participant share what each part symbolizes and put them on display.

Variations:

⇒   Vary the theme from family to some other relevant theme.
⇒   For very large groups, have participants break into groups of 4-6 when conducting step 3 above.

| **Materials**: For each table: clay, paper, markers, tape, toilet paper rolls, plastic eyes, felt, pipe cleaners, fabric, etc. | **Setup**: Tables | **Group Size**: Any size |

A3   Advertising Who I Am!

| **Goal**: Starter | **Ages**: 6-Adult | **Time**: 15 minutes |

Directions:

1. Give each participant a sheet of tag board and supplies.
2. Tell each group they are to create their own advertisement for a product to represent who they are and where they want to go with their life.
3. When finished, have some participants share the products with the entire group.

| **Materials**: For each participant: Tag board, markers, glue, glitter, ribbon, other common decorating items | **Setup**: Tables or desks | **Group Size**: Any size |

A4   Who Are You Anyway?

| **Goal**: Starter | **Ages**: 10-Adult | **Time**: 10-15 minutes |

Directions:

1. Each participant should write his/her first and last names on a name tag.
2. Each participant should pair up with another person in the room and spend one minute each telling the other everything they can about themselves.
3. When two minutes has expired, the participants in each pair should exchange name tags. The participants will now chose a different partner. This time, however, the participants will introduce themselves as the person whose name tag they are wearing and using all the information that was told to them by their previous partner.
4. Continue this process for three more turns.
5. At the end of the 5th sharing turn, stop the sharing and instruct each participant to find the person who possesses their name tag and introduce themselves to the person. The person who possesses the name tag should then introduce him/herself as if he/she were that person. Find out how much of the information was accurate and how much was lost in the sharing.

Variations:

⇒ Have the 5th name tag holder introduce the person whose name tag is being worn to the entire group.
⇒ Specific questions could be asked of each person, such as favorite foods, music groups, etc.

| **Materials**: Name tags, safety pins, pens or pencils | **Setup**: None | **Group Size**: Any size |

A5   Gifts I Bring

Goal: Starter	**Ages**: 8-Adult	**Time**: 3-5 minutes

Directions:

1. Give each participant a "Gift Card" (see Illustration A5).
2. Have each participant write one positive thing each brings to this session (or will take from the session when using this activity for "Closure") on their gift card.
3. Each participant should pair up with a partner and share the gift.
4. Each participant should then introduce their partner to the entire group and share the gift they brought to the session (or will take from the session when using this activity for "Closure").

Variations:

⇒   A large gift box could be placed in the room and each card put in the box as a reminder of the gifts given or received.
⇒   This activity can also be used for "Closure."

Materials: 1 "Gift Card" (see illustration) and a pen or pencil for each participant	**Setup**: None	**Group Size**: Any size, divided into pairs

Illustration A5: Gift Card

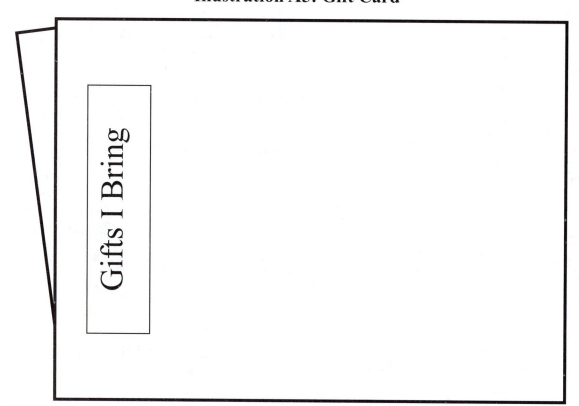

A6   You Probably Didn't Know

| **Goal**: Starter | **Ages**: 6-Adult | **Time**: 10 minutes |

Directions:

1. Have participants sit in chairs in a circle.
2. Give participants time to think about something most people don't know about them.
3. Have the leader share something to model the activity. Such as:
   - ⇒ You probably didn't know my parents live in Alaska.
   - ⇒ You probably didn't know that I write music.
   - ⇒ You probably didn't know that my sister is a writer.
4. After each participant has had a turn, discuss whether or not knowledge makes a difference in relationships.

Variations:

⇒ If participants are meeting to discuss or learn about a specific topic, focus the sharing on this topic. For example, if the students are meeting to learn about leadership, have each participant share a leadership experience he/she had.

| **Materials**: None | **Setup**: Chairs in a circle | **Group Size**: 5-20 participants |

A7   What Shape Are You?

| **Goal**: Starter | **Ages**: 5-Adult | **Time**: 10 minutes |

Directions:

1. For a welcome warmup during a first session, cut squares from colored paper. You will need one square for every two participants.
2. Cut each square into two irregular shapes and put them in a box or hat.
3. Ask each participant to choose a shape.
4. Have each participant find the person that possesses the missing part of the square.
5. Let the "new friends" get acquainted for a few minutes.

Variations:

⇒ Have the new pairs introduce each other to the group.

| **Materials**: Pieces of colored paper, scissors | **Setup**: None | **Group Size**: 6-18 participants |

| **Goal**: Starter | **Ages**: 8-Adult | **Time**: 10-15 minutes |

Directions:

1. Prior to the beginning of the session, copy the shoe and footprint illustration (A8) for each participant.
2. Divide the participants into groups of about five and distribute a worksheet and a pencil to each participant.
3. Ask each participant to write on the sole of their shoe how their "sole" is feeling right now.
4. On the tongue of the shoe have participants, show how they are feeling when they talk to others.
5. On the insole of the shoe, have each participant write a supportive feeling each has about the group.
6. Next, have participants turn to the footprint illustration. Tell the participants that when they leave the activity, they may want to leave something behind (e.g., pleasant memory, wish for the group). Ask the participants to write on the footprint something each would like to leave behind.
7. Allow time for participants to share their shoe and footprint with their group.

| **Materials**: A pencil and a shoe footprint worksheet (see illustration) for each participant | **Setup**: None | **Group Size**: Any size, divided into groups of about 5 |

Illustration A8: Shoes of the Present, Footprints Left Behind

Shoe

Footprint

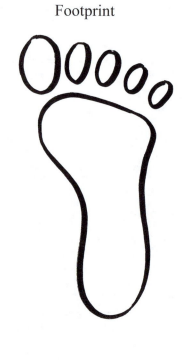

A9 My Personalized License Plate

| **Goal**: Starter | **Ages**: 8-Adult | **Time**: 15 minutes |

Directions:

1. Divide participants into groups of about five.
2. Ask the group to think of unique license plates they have seen. Discuss why license plates use landmarks and symbols (team insignia, animals, etc.).
3. Tell each participant to develop a personalized license plate using whatever symbol (s) each feels appropriate.
4. Have participants share the license plates among group members.

| **Materials**: Markers, glitter, glue, scissors, and other decorating materials, 1 copy of illustration A9 per participant | **Setup**: Tables and chairs | **Group Size**: Any size, divided into groups of about 5 |

= = = = = = = = = = = = = =

Illustration A9: My Personalized License Plate

A10   Groupmate Search

Goal: Starter	Ages: 7-10	Time: 30-40 minutes

Directions:

1. Prior to the beginning of the session the facilitator will need to construct a "Groupmate Search" worksheet, similar to illustration A10, using the names of the group participants.
2. At the beginning of a session, tell participants they are going to try to match other participants to the names on the list.
3. Distribute one "Groupmate Search" to each participant and ask the participants to match as many people with names as they can. (Allow no more than ten minutes.) A participant must meet and greet a participant prior to highlighting their name in the search grid.
4. Next, have participants find at least three people they have already met and reveal one thing about themselves.
5. Finally, have participants quickly introduce one participant they talked to and share one detail about that person. Use the overhead and highlighter to keep track of who has had a turn.

Materials: A "Groupmate Search" sheet (roster of all participants in the group similar to illustration A10) for each participant, a pencil, large poster or overhead transparency with names of all the group participants on it, highlighter	Setup: None	Group Size: Up to about 20 participants

---

Illustration A10: Sample Groupmate Search

```
PRORICHARDZN
DMYNIQHPTEAR
CHRISTOPHERR
OASKGHAOERAM
VNZKAOMBGIPD
RROIFMATTCAR
TIEQZASAMKTI
NJKRJSKWDWRA
EMXQBECAFUIN
YLGEOQLNANCO
```

A11   Painting a Picture of Me

Goal: Starter	**Ages**: 7-10 years	**Time**: 15 minutes

Directions:

1. Distribute the markers, crayons and "Painting a Picture of Me" illustration (A11) to each participant.
2. Instruct participants to color the puzzle pieces in the color that best represents how they feel about that activity, using the color code on the illustration sheet.
3. At the end of the activity, have students share their "painted" pictures with the person next to them.

Materials: One copy of illustration A11 "Painting a Picture of Me" for each participant, crayons, markers	**Setup**: None	**Group Size**: Any size

Illustration A11: Painting a Picture of Me

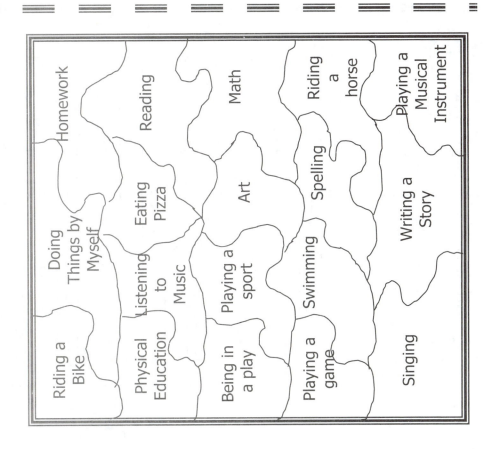

Green: Really Like
Red: Kind of like
Blue: Don't like
Yellow: Really don't like

Homework
Reading
Math
Riding a horse
Playing a Musical Instrument
Doing Things by Myself
Eating Pizza
Art
Spelling
Writing a Story
Riding a Bike
Listening to Music
Playing a sport
Swimming
Physical Education
Being in a play
Playing a game
Singing

A12   It's Out of the Bag

Goal: Starter	**Ages**: 6-10 years	**Time**: 5-10 minutes

Directions:

1. Before the session begins, write participants' names on the illustration (A12), cut them apart, and put the strips in a bag.
2. Be sure all participants have been introduced and are wearing name tags.
3. Have participants sit in a circle and pass the bag around while music plays in the background.
4. In the tradition of musical chairs, stop the music periodically and have the person holding the bag pull out a card and follow the directions on the card.
5. Continue as time allows.

Materials: Medium sized bag, strips about group (see illustration A12), music, tape recorder or something else to play music	**Setup**: Room for participants to sit in a circle	**Group Size**: Any size

Illustration A12: It's Out of the Bag

Directions: The following sentence strips need to have the names filled in before the game starts.

Find out if _____ has any pets.

Find out what _____ 's favorite song is.

Find out if _____ likes beets.

Find out if _____ has ever ridden a horse.

Find out if _____ has eaten Chinese food.

Find out if _____ has ever played chess.

Find out if _____ plays a musical instrument.

Find out if _____ likes country music.

Find out if _____ likes to get up early.

Find out what _____ 's favorite color is.

Find out if _____ has a sister.

Find out if _____ has eaten seaweed.

Find out if _____ has a snake.

Find out if _____ has gone to an amusement park.

Find out if _____ likes funny movies.

Find out if _____ likes winter or summer best.

Find out if _____ wants to be in a school play.

Find out if _____ has been to the Grand Canyon.

Find out if _____ likes to read adventure stories.

Find out if _____ has seen a movie in the last two weeks.

Find out if _____ likes chocolate cake.

Find out if _____ can make a paper airplane.

Find out if _____ likes to play video games.

Find out if _____ 's grandmother lives less than 50 miles away.

Find out if _____ enjoys outdoor activities.

A13   All About Me

| **Goal**: Starter | **Ages**: 5-Adult | **Time**: 10-15 minutes |

Directions:

1. Tell participants to make name tags that best represent them.
2. Their name is to be written in the center of the card and other symbols should be drawn on the card that best describe who each is.
3. Have each participant punch the card and tie yarn for a hang tag while discussing their name tags and what the symbols represent.

| **Materials**: 2' lengths of yarn, markers, crayons, stickers, other decoration materials, index cards, hole punch | **Setup**: Tables | **Group Size**: Any size |

A14   Name Your Shape

| **Goal**: Starter | **Ages**: 6-Adult | **Time**: 5-10 minutes |

Directions:

1. Give each participant a sheet of construction paper, a piece of string, and a marker.
2. Instruct participants to create their own name tag by tearing their paper into a shape (such as a triangle, car, etc.) that is symbolic of them.
3. Have each participant write his/her name on the tag.
4. Punch holes at each corner of the name tag, pull the string through each hole and tie the two ends of their string together.
5. Tell participants to put the name tag around their necks.
6. Instruct participants to sit in the circle and introduce themselves using their name tag creations. Have each explain how the shape of the tag is symbolic of him/her.

Variations:

⇒ Have participants pair up, share their name and meaning of their name tag shape to their partner, and introduce each other to the group upon returning to the circle.
⇒ Have each participant share one thing they would like to learn from the group meeting.

| **Materials**: Construction paper (1 sheet per participant - 4" x 6" minimum), string (1 length per participant - 35" minimum), markers, and a hole punch. | **Setup**: Room to circulate and sit in a circle | **Group Size**: Any size |

A15   A Look at Our Group

Goal: Starter	**Ages**: 8-Adult	**Time**: 10 minutes

Directions:

1. Prior to the beginning of the session, prepare and place the illustrated charts on the wall.
2. Instruct participants to place a sticker on the approximate place on the chart to represent information about themselves.

Materials: Charts 1-5 (see Illustration A15), colored sticker dots	**Setup**: None	**Group Size**: Any size

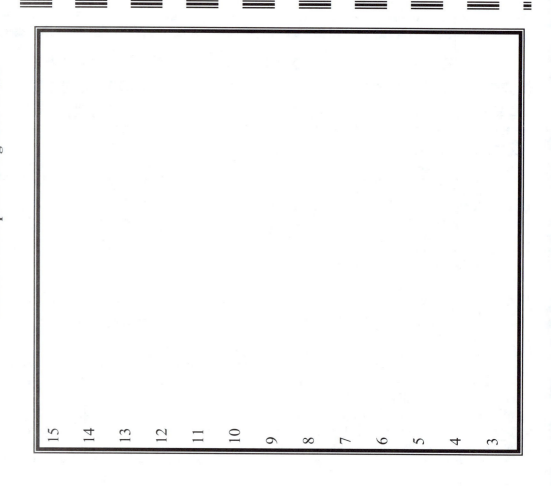

Illustration A15: A Look at Our Group

Chart One

Hours of Computer Usage Per Week

15 14 13 12 11 10 9 8 7 6 5 4 3

Illustration A15 (continued)

Chart Three

Number of Siblings in Your Family

0	1	2
3	4	Other

Illustration A15 (continued)

Chart Two

Hair and Eye Color Chart

HAIR COLOR

	RED	BROWN	BLACK	BLOND	WHITE/GRAY
EYE COLOR BLUE					
GREEN					
BROWN					
HAZEL					

13

Illustration A15 (continued)

Chart Five

Favorite Types of Ice Cream

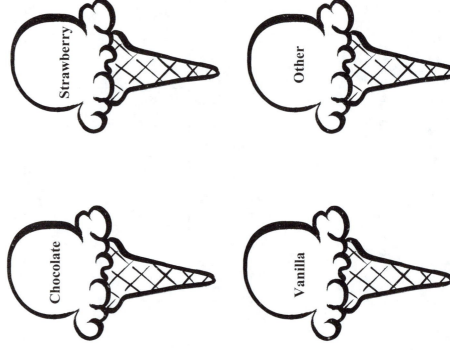

Illustration A15 (continued)

Chart Four

Favorite Types of Movies

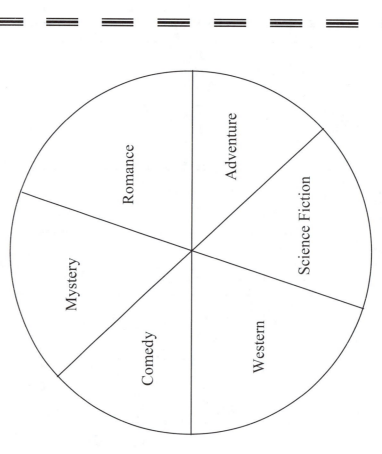

A16   Mission Possible

| Goal: Starter | Ages: 8-Adult | Time: 5-10 minutes |

Directions:

1. Distribute the "Mission Possible" sheet and a pen/pencil to each participant.
2. Tell the group they are on a "mission" to find out information about their group.
3. Allow 5-10 minutes for the group to mingle, find and identify participants with the indicated characteristics, and complete as much of the sheet as they can.

Variations:

⇒ Participants can turn in their sheet and a drawing can be held with prizes.

| Materials: One "Mission Possible" sheet (see Illustration A16) and pen or pencil per participant | Setup: None | Group Size: Any size |

Illustration A16: Mission Possible

Try to find someone who fits each of these descriptions, then ask that person to sign the line. Even if you don't fill all the lines, see how many different names you can get--and how many new friends you make. You may even find out something new about an old friend.

FIND SOMEONE WHO...

1. is taller than you_____
2. is left-handed_____
3. walks to school_____
4. has curly hair_____
5. has no sisters or brothers_____
6. has initials that repeat_____
7. was born in your town_____
8. is new to your school_____
9. went camping this summer_____
10. is the oldest child_____
11. has an unusual pet_____
12. has a collection of something_____
13. has brown eyes_____
14. was in your class last year_____
15. is on a sports team_____
16. has been to Disney World_____
17. has an 8 letter name_____
18. has broken a bone_____

19. has freckles_____
20. has a birthday this month_____
21. has traveled to at least 5 states_____
22. has long hair_____
23. was born in another country_____
24. wears glasses_____
25. takes music lessons_____
26. can whistle_____
27. just moved to a new home_____
28. has seen 2 oceans_____
29. is the youngest child_____
30. rides a bus to school_____
31. has been a hospital patient_____
32. read a book this summer_____
33. has red hair_____
34. has a tooth missing_____
35. has eaten a strange food_____
36. hasn't met you before_____

A17   Fortune Extras

Goal: Starter	**Ages**: 8-Adult	**Time**: 15-20 minutes

Directions:

1. Before the session begins, wrap each cookie with a strip cut from the illustration (A17) and a piece of tape.
2. Divide the participants into groups of 4 or more.
3. Have each group sit in a circle and give each person a cookie.
4. Go around the circle and allow participants to take turns opening their cookies and answering the questions or following the directions on their slip of paper.

Materials: Fortune cookies (or other cookies), scissors, small strips of paper from the "Fortune Extras" illustration A17, tape	**Setup**: None	**Group Size**: Any size, divided into groups of at least 4

Illustration A17: Fortune Extras

State three things you like about your group.

Give a compliment to everyone in your group.

What do you feel is your best group skill?

What is one thing that makes you feel good about your group?

What is the best thing that has happened in the group?

Name someone in the group who makes you feel good.

Name the person who is the leader in the group.

A18   Layer by Layer

| **Goal**: Starter | **Ages**: 8-Adult | **Time**: 10-15 minutes |

Directions:

1. Give each participant a copy of the Layer by Layer worksheet (Illustration A18).
2. Tell participants to read the directions at the bottom and have other group members fill in the spaces by signing or initialing the appropriate spaces each can claim.
3. Participants should introduce themselves as they meet others.

| **Materials**: One Layer by Layer worksheet (see Illustration A18) per participant | **Setup**: None | **Group Size**: Any size |

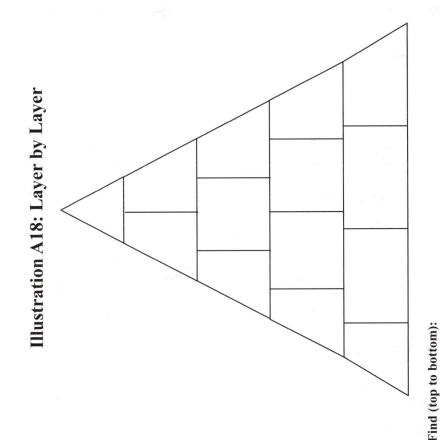

Illustration A18: Layer by Layer

Find (top to bottom):

Layer 1- Person who has gone out of the country in the past year

Layer 2- People who went out of state in the past year

Layer 3- People who made something in the past year

Layer 4- People who have read 5 or more books in the past year

Layer 5- People who have been in a workshop or other session during the past year

A19   A w a r d   C e r e m o n y

Goal: Starter	**Ages**: 10-Adult	**Time**: 10 minutes

Directions:

1. Distribute the ribbons and markers to participants.
2. Have each participant think about one achievement during the session (group of sessions, during the past year, etc.) to be proud of.
3. Each participant should write their name and the accomplishment on the ribbon.
4. Invite each participant to put the ribbon on their clothing (using the tape) and wear it the rest of the session.

Variations:

⇒   Have participants walk around the room, read each other's accomplishments and introduce themselves by name.

⇒   This activity can also be used for "Closure."

⇒   Have the group suggest accomplishments or strengths for each participant to write on the ribbon.

Materials: 1 blue ribbon (see Illustration A19) and 1 marker for each participant. One roll of masking tape	**Setup**: None	**Group Size**: Any size

Illustration A19: Blue ribbon for the "Award Ceremony" activity

A20 Yarning to Know About You!

Goal: Starter	Ages: 5-Adult	Time: 15-20 minutes

Directions:

1. Tell the participants they will get to know each other.
2. Demonstrate the activity as you give directions.
3. Pick a piece of yarn from a box (or top of a table, etc.) and tell about yourself as you wind the yarn around your finger. Do not stop talking until the yarn is completely wrapped around your finger.
4. Ask for volunteers to come to the front of the group, pick a piece of yarn, and tell the group about themselves. Participants are to talk until their yarn runs out.
5. Do as many "yarns" as time allows.

Note: You may have to prompt younger participants about what to say (Tell us about your pets, favorite foods, music, etc.)

Materials: 1 piece of yarn per participant. The length of the yarn should vary from 1' to 3'	Setup: None	Group Size: Any size

---

A21 Glad to Meet You

Goal: Starter	Ages: 6-Adult	Time: 5-10 minutes

Directions:

1. Enlist a volunteer from the audience.
2. Demonstrate with the volunteer several types of handshakes.
3. Tell participants they are going to create unique handshakes for 3 purposes:
    a. get acquainted handshake
    b. an energizer handshake
    c. you did it handshake
4. Designate three areas of the room and have participants count off by threes to assign them to a group.
5. Have each group develop the designated handshake. Give each group 3 minutes.
6. Then have participants go around the room introducing themselves to other participants with their new handshakes.

Variations:

⇒ Change names of handshakes to suit the audience or purpose of the group meeting.

Materials: None	Setup: A room that allows for some movement	Group Size: More than 10 participants

A22 "Leafing" Angry Thoughts Behind

| **Goal**: Starter | **Ages**: 5-Adult | **Time**: 8-10 minutes |

Directions:

1. Pass out three different leaves to each participant.
2. Play the calming music and remind participants that anger is often a part of our daily lives and can affect our health, work/school, and family lives. Now it is time to see how we can reduce our level of anger.
3. Ask participants to identify three things that really anger them and write one of these things on each leaf.
4. Remind participants that whatever the season of the year, we can always turn over a "new leaf" and make changes in our lives.
5. Ask participants to think about what it would take to "turn over a new leaf." Ask participants to turn over their leaves and write one way to reduce the negative aspects of the thing on the other side of the leaf that makes them angry.
6. When participants have finished, tell them they now have options to "releaf" their anger. Encourage them to look at the leaves each day, front and back, to remind them to work on the things that cause them anger.

Variations:

⇒ Share with partners and brainstorm other ways to work on the anger.
⇒ Designate one leaf each for family, work/school, and social relationships.

| **Materials**: 3 leaves for each participant (see Illustration A22), markers or pencils, calming music (played in the background) | **Setup**: None | **Group Size**: Any size |

Illustration A22: "Leafing" Angry Thoughts Behind

A23	Tic-Tac-Toe

Goal: Starter	**Ages**: 7-10 years	**Time**: 8 minutes

Directions:

1. Pass out blank tic-tac-toe grids to each person in the group.
2. Have each person go around the room and collect nine signatures, one in each of the nine tic-tac-toe spaces.
3. Tell all participants to return to their seats.
4. Give the rules of the game. The first one to complete a row in any direction (horizontal, vertical, diagonal) is the winner.
5. The facilitator randomly calls out the names of people in the group one at a time until someone calls out tic-tac-toe.

Materials: Tic-tac-toe grid (see Illustration A23), pencils	**Setup**: None	**Group Size**: Any size

Illustration A23: Tic-Tac-Toe Grid

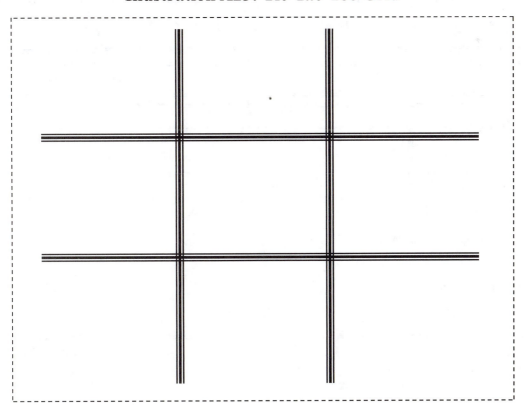

A24   Gold Medal Time

| **Goal**: Starter | **Ages**: 8-Adult | **Time**: 15 minutes |

Directions:

1. Before beginning the activity, cut out a 3" cardboard circle for each participant.
2. Have the participants put their name in the center of the circle.
3. Ask the participants to put things they are proud of around their name.
4. Have each participant decorate the paper medal.
5. Have participants share their pride and accomplishments with the group.

Variations:

⇒ If the group is more than 15, consider dividing the participants into smaller groups for the sharing portion.

| **Materials**: 3-inch cardboard circles, ribbon, stickers, markers | **Setup**: None | **Group Size**: Any size |

A25   The Sharing Hands

| **Goal**: Starter | **Ages**: 8-Adult | **Time**: 10 minutes |

Directions:

1. Invite participants to find a partner.
2. Instruct each participant to trace his/her partner's handprint on the piece of construction paper. Both partner's handprints should fit on the sheet of paper.
3. Have each participant write his/her name on the inside of their handprint near the bottom of the palm.
4. Explain that participants are to take a few minutes to interview each other about strengths or interests. Write 1 point of interest/strength on each of the five fingers. Each participant should be interviewing their partner and writing on their partner's hand simultaneously.
5. At the end of five minutes share the details with the other participants.
6. Hang up the finished products.

Variations:

⇒ Have participants write five wishes for their group or organization.

| **Materials**: 12" x 18" colored construction paper (1 sheet for each pair), markers, tape | **Setup**: None | **Group Size**: Any size, divided into pairs |

A26   Introductions Again?

Goal: Starter   **Ages**: 8-Adult   **Time**: 10-15 minutes

Directions:
1. After participants have worked with each other for at least one session, have groups do this activity.
2. Group members should introduce themselves by nicknames they have been given and explain how the nickname was derived. Each group member should fill out a card with their nickname and wear it for the rest of the session.

Variations:
⇒ This activity can be the opener for another self-disclosure-type activity.

Materials: Index cards, markers, yarn, hole punch   **Setup**: None   **Group Size**: Any size

---

A27   The Key Is Use

Goal: Starter   **Ages**: Adults   **Time**: 5 minutes

Directions:
1. Ask participants to find a partner.
2. All of us carry keys with us to open places we need to enter.
3. Ask participants to get out the keys they have with them. Tell them they each have one minute to introduce themselves and to explain the purpose of their keys to their partner.
4. After 2 minutes, ask participants to raise their hands if they have a key on their ring that they don't use. Have participants discuss what other characteristics or talents each may have that are often or seldom used.

Materials: None   **Setup**: None   **Group Size**: Any size

A28　　　Participant Tree

Goal: Starter | **Ages**: 5-Adult | **Time**: 5 minutes

Directions:

1. Before the session begins, cut out one leaf for each participant and draw a tree on the large sheet of paper (you can use the leaves included in Illustration A22).
2. On one wall of the room, tape the picture of the tree.
3. Distribute a leaf to each participant.
4. Have each participant put their name on the leaf and one personal fact each would like the group to know.
5. Have each participant introduce him/herself, share the fact/detail, and tape the leaf on the Participant Tree.

Variations:

⇒ Vary the information you want the participant to disclose (e.g., one thing you learned today, two things that make you happy, etc.)

Materials: Large piece of paper with a tree drawn on it, paper leaves for each participant, markers, tape.

Setup: Large wall to place the tree drawing

Group Size: Any size

A29　　Look at My Button!

Goal: Starter | **Ages**: 8-Adult | **Time**: 5-10 minutes

Directions:

1. Divide the participants into groups of about 4.
2. Distribute materials to each group and have each group cut a large circular shape from the paper.
3. Have the group design a button with a positive message according to the topic you assign (get acquainted, topic of the session, etc,)
4. Let each group discuss and share their buttons with the other groups.

Materials: Colored paper, scissors, markers, straight pins

Setup: Tables

Group Size: Any size, divided ino groups of about 4

Section B

Energizers

B 1   It's Snowing!

| **Goal**: Energizer | **Ages**: 8-Adult | **Time**: 3-5 minutes |

Directions:

1. Pass out scissors and a sheet of paper to each participant.
2. Instruct participants to make a snowflake by folding and cutting the paper. (Demonstrate if needed.)
3. Explain to participants that they are to introduce themselves to as many people as they can, giving their names, showing their snowflake to each person they meet and sharing one thing about themselves that is unique or different.
4. When they finish their conversation, participants should exchange snowflakes and meet someone else.
5. After about four minutes, ask participants to share some of the unique and different descriptions they heard.

Variations:

⇒   Use flowers or stars instead of snowflakes.

⇒   Ask participants to write about an event they remember from their childhood on the snowflake and share it with other participants.

| **Materials**: Scissors and 1 piece of paper (about 5" x 5") for each participant | **Setup**: None | **Group Size**: 10 or more participants |

B 2   Good for You!

| **Goal**: Energizer | **Ages**: 8-Adult | **Time**: 5 minutes |

Directions:

1. Explain to the group that there is a certain joy in each of us when we celebrate.
2. Instruct participants to go around the room and meet as many people as they can. After they introduce themselves, they should offer a congratulatory statement. If the participants cannot think of a genuine congratulatory statement, it is OK to "make one up," such as "It's great that we won the basketball game last week," or "You're the first person to make it to the big leagues without trying out! Great job!"
3. Explain that each participant should try to meet as many people in this manner as possible.
4. Allow 3-4 minutes for this activity.
5. Have several participants share how it felt to give and receive such hearty congratulations.

| **Materials**: None | **Setup**: Space to move around | **Group Size**: 10 or more participants |

B3　　　　Heat It Up

| **Goal**: Energizer | **Ages**: 8-Adult | **Time**: 15-20 minutes |

Directions:

1. Divide the participants into groups of 4-6.
2. Tell the groups they are to brainstorm as many uses of an old stove (or some other common object) as possible. Each group should put all their ideas on newsprint.
3. Share the ideas with the entire group.

| **Materials**: Newsprint, markers | **Setup**: None | **Group Size**: 12 or more participants |

B4　　　Please Pass the Hoop

| **Goal**: Energizer | **Ages**: 5-Adult | **Time**: 10 minutes |

Directions:

1. Tell participants that each group should clasp hands and form a straight line.
2. Put a hoop around the neck of the first person in the line and explain to the participants that the goal is for each group to get the hoop to the other end of the line without anyone unclasping hands.
3. Groups should be given three minutes to brainstorm and decide how to accomplish the task.
4. The facilitator then begins the race and the group that finishes first is the winner.
5. As a group, have participants discuss what team behaviors and comments were helpful and unhelpful.

Variations:

⇒　Have participants discuss methods for speeding up their performance for three minutes and have each group try again.
⇒　This activity can also be used for "Team Building" and as a "Starter."

| **Materials**: 1 hula hoop for each team | **Setup**: Large open space | **Group Size**: 12–50 divided into groups of equal numbers of participants (6-10 participants is optimal, but no more than 10 on each team) |

B5   We Are Siamese

Goal: Energizer	**Ages**: 8-Adult	**Time**: 10 minutes

Directions:

1. Set up an obstacle course that "Siamese Twins" teams can maneuver through. A sample course is provided in the illustration.
2. Relay teams should be formed with at least six participants per team. An even number of participants should comprise each team. Team members will pair up and tie their legs together with a cloth strip (one participant's left leg tied to their partner's right leg, like in a traditional three-legged race).
3. The goal of the relay is for the teams (one pair at a time and using only their feet) to maneuver the ball around the 3 obstacle cones (chairs) and back to the start/finish line. The first complete team to maneuver the course is the winner.

Variations:

⇒   Have the participants discuss ways of improving performance to overcome barriers and obstacles, then repeat the race.
⇒   This activity can also be used as a "Starter."

Materials: 3 obstacle cones (or chairs) per team, a marked start/finish line, 1 plastic or playground ball per team, one 3' long cloth strip per pair	**Setup**: See illustration B5	**Group Size**: 12 or more, divided into teams of at least 6, then into pairs

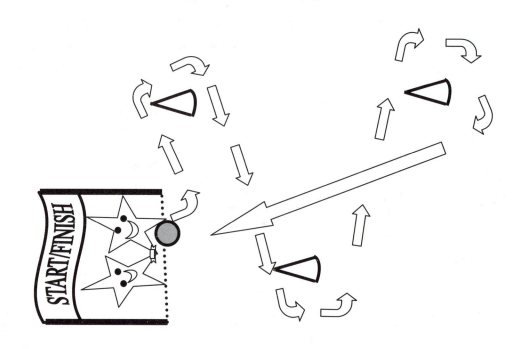

Illustration B5: Obstacle course for the "We Are Siamese" activity

B 6   Can O' Worms

Goal: Energizer	**Ages**: 13-Adult	**Time**: 15-20 minutes

Directions:

1. Divide participants into pairs and have one participant from each pair pull a piece of yarn from the can, but not reveal the contents written on the paper.
2. Explain that since no one in the room knows the identity of their famous couple, each pair will have to act out a routine that will illustrate the couple's identity, but without revealing the names.
3. Each couple will have 3-5 minutes to create and rehearse a routine.
4. After the rehearsal, have each couple perform the routine. Encourage all participants to guess the names of the famous couple.

Variations:

⇒ Have the couples mime the routines.
⇒ Encourage participants to create and use props.
⇒ Give prizes to each couple for their courage and skill.
⇒ This activity can also be used for "Team Building," or as a "Starter" if the participants are asked to give some basic information after completing a routine.

Materials: 1 large can, 1 card for every 2 participants containing the names of a famous couple with a 1 foot long piece of yarn tied through a hole in each card. (See the illustration B6 for a list of some famous couples to consider.)	**Setup**: None	**Group Size**: Any size, but best with smaller groups

Illustration B6: Can O' Worms

○ Bert & Ernie	○ Romeo & Juliet
○ Darth Vader & Luke Skywalker	○ Charlie Brown & Lucy
○ Santa & Ruldolph	○ Dorothy & the Scarecrow
○ Snow White & Prince	○ Lone Ranger & Tonto
○ Peter Pan & Tinkerbell	○ Jack & Jill
○ Red Riding Hood & Big Bad Wolf	○ Tarzan & Jane
○ Sonny & Cher	○ Rocky & Bullwinkle
○ Batman & Robin	○ Bonnie & Clyde

Any other examples can be used

B7	**Throwing It All Away**

Goal: Energizer	**Ages**: 6-Adult	**Time**: 3-5 minutes

Directions:

1. Put a large, empty can and several containers each with candy, pencils, or scraps of paper in the middle of each table.
2. Tell participants it is important to get rid of negative thoughts and keep a clear mind.
3. Explain the topics for the session.
4. Ask participants to take some scrap paper from the table at any time throughout the day and write any negative thoughts about the topic or anything else on the paper.
5. Instruct participants to wad up the paper and put the paper in the empty can. They should keep track of the number of trash pieces they throw.
6. As a reward, tell participants they can take as many pieces of candy from the container as the number of negative thoughts they threw into the can.

Materials: For each table provide 1 large, empty, open top can, a container with candy, a container with scraps of paper, and a cup with several pens or pencils	**Setup**: Tables and chairs	**Group Size**: 8-30 participants

B8	**Wagon Ho!**

Goal: Energizer	**Ages**: 8-Adult	**Time**: 5-8 minutes

Directions:

1. Distribute two deflated balloons of different colors to each participant.
2. Divide participants into groups of about six and tell each group they are a wagon train that picks up passengers along the trail. Two passengers (balloons) per participant are allowed.
3. Explain that the balloons become passengers when a participant inflates and draws a face on them with a marker.
4. Tell each team to move in wagon train formation (one behind the other with their hands on the shoulders or waist of the team member in front of them) to a location where there is another participant from another train with a balloon of the desired color. In order to collect the balloon from the other participant, one must introduce themselves and offer a compliment or insight gained about the day's topic.
5. Each participant must inflate two balloons of the same color, tie them together with the string, and draw a face on each with the marker. That person carries the passenger with them. Each part of the wagon train (person) needs to pick up two passengers (balloons of the same color) although different group members may choose different balloon colors.
6. Trains must stay still while one person inflates a balloon and draws a face on it.
7. The groups will be competing to fill their wagon trains. By the end of the activity, each participant should have two balloons of the same color. The wagon train that is filled with passengers first is the winner.

Materials: Two deflated balloons of the same color and a 3' length of string per participant and one permanent marker per group	**Setup**: A large open area	**Group Size**: 20-100, divided into groups of about 6 participants

B9 Look Again!

| Goal: Energizer | Ages: 6-Adult | Time: 10 minutes |

Directions:

1. Have 6-10 participants sit in a circle.
2. Ask one of the participants to volunteer to be the observer. The observer will watch the members of the group for one minute.
3. The observer then will leave the room and the remaining participants will make changes in the way or place each was seated. This should take no longer than 30 seconds.
4. The observer then will come back in the room and attempt to guess what changes took place.
5. Once the observer has guessed the changes, select another observer who will watch the group for 30 seconds and then leave the room for 30 seconds.
6. This time only 3 people in the group should make a change.
7. The 2nd observer will come back and identify the change.
8. Continue as long as time allows.

Variations:

⇒ The observer can make a change after leaving the room and the group can guess the change.
⇒ Have the group all make the same change.
⇒ Ask the observer to identify things that helped him/her to remember.

| Materials: None | Setup: None | Group Size: Any size |

B10 Let's Move Together

| Goal: Energizer | Ages: 5-Adult | Time: 5 minutes at the beginning and 30 seconds—1 minute for each group later in the session |

Directions:

1. Divide participants into groups of 6-20. Give each group a number.
2. Tell the groups to develop a synchronized movement of some sort as a group.
3. Allow them to brainstorm for one minute. (Play music in the background).
4. Have the groups practice their movements (2 minutes).
5. Tell the groups at various times during the session a group number will be called and that group will present their synchronized movement to the entire group.

Variations:

⇒ Give each group a movement to perform.

| Materials: Music, CD/tape player | Setup: None | Group Size: Any size, divided into groups of 6-20 |

B11   Give It Up!

Goal: Energizer	**Ages**: 5-Adult	**Time**: 30 secs-2 min for each activity

Directions:

1. Before the session begins, cut out activity slips.
2. Give one to each of the 1ˢᵗ 15 participants to enter the room. Explain that sometime during the presentation, they will have to lead the group in the activity listed on their slip.
3. During the session, call a topic by the number and let the activities begin.

Note: Give directions on the slips if you feel they are needed.

Materials: Music, activity slips (see illustration B11)	**Setup**: Large, open area	**Group Size**: Any size

Illustration B11: Give It Up!

1. Swimming
2. Kick line
3. Round of row, row your boat
4. Directing traffic
5. YMCA
6. Lead a cheer
7. The wave
8. The twist
9. Jogging in place
10. Neck circles
11. Driving down the road
12. Stretching
13. Arm circles
14. Jumping jacks
15. Hitchhike movement

32

B12   What Are They Here For?

Goal: Energizer	**Ages**: 5-Adult	**Time**: Begin this activity half way through the session

Directions:

1. Before the session begins, place 3 pipe cleaners at each participant's seat. Don't tell the participants what the pipe cleaners are to be used for until about halfway through the session.
2. Tell participants at each table they are to make any kind of sculpture out of the pipe cleaners. Urge them to be very creative.
3. Ask the participants at each table to select a winner. Give each winner a prize.
4. Give special recognition to groups who combined their pipe cleaners to build a group structure.

Materials: 3 pipe cleaners per participant, prizes	**Setup**: Tables	**Group Size**: Any size

---

B13   Everybody Swings

Goal: Energizer	**Ages**: 5-Adult	**Time**: 2-3 minutes

Directions:

1. Participants should be standing around in a large circle.
2. Demonstrate the process in country dancing of linking and releasing arms at the elbow and circling around from one participant to the next. Have the group practice linking and releasing arms to the left and to the right.
3. Explain that in this activity, they'll get to know people in a short amount of time.
4. Tell them when the music begins they should move around the circle, introducing themselves by their first name only, saying "Hi, I'm _____." Stop the music periodically to allow pairs to have a 15–30 second conversation on a topic of your choice.

Materials: Country music	**Setup**: Large open space	**Group Size**: Any size

B14 I Know You From Every Side

| **Goal**: Energizer | **Ages**: 8-Adult | **Time**: 5 minutes |

Directions:

1. Ask participants to stand in an open area where there is lots of room to move around.
2. Explain the rules and demonstrate the activity.

⇒   When I blow the whistle and call out "one side" each participant should find a partner.

⇒   I will give instructions: side-by-side, back-to-back, face-to-face. Partners should position themselves accordingly.

⇒   When the partners are positioned side-by-side, they should introduce themselves giving their name, where they live and the number of brothers and sisters they have. When they are back-to-back, they should tell their favorite activities. When face-to-face, they should tell about their favorite movies and type of music.

⇒   When "On all sides" is called out, four participants should gather together and discuss a current event.

Tips: Use a poster with directions so everyone remembers what to do!

| **Materials**: Whistle | **Setup**: Open space | **Group Size**: 10 or more partici- pants |

B15   Balloon Team Olympics

| **Goal**: Energizer | **Ages**: 5-Adult | **Time**: 10-15 minutes |

Directions:

1. In a large room, mark starting and finishing lines about 25 feet apart.
2. Divide participants into teams of an even number, and further divide the team members into pairs.
3. Participants should line up as partner sets, one pair behind the other pairs of their team.
4. Give each participant a balloon. Have each participant blow up the balloon and tie it so it stays inflated.
5. Explain the following rules to the group:
   - A. This is a relay race and the goal is for the team to work together and finish first.
   - B. As each pair moves to the front of the line, they should put the two balloons between them and hold them there without touching them with their hands. (Each pair needs to decide how to hold their balloons, for example, side-to-side, back-to-back, etc.)
   - C. In turn, have each pair walk toward the end of the line and then back to the starting line without dropping their balloons.
   - D. When one pair comes back to the starting line, another pair may start.
   - E. If a balloon escapes, the pair must stop and start again.
6. After the competition ends, lead a discussion of the factors that facilitated good teamwork.

Note: This is meant to be great fun, not a serious competition.

| **Materials**: One balloon per partici- pant (plus several extra) | **Setup**: Large open room | **Group Size**: 20 or more, divided into even number teams and further divided into pairs |

B16   Teeth Rule!

Goal: Energizer	**Ages**: 6-Adult	**Time**: 10-15 mintes

Directions:

1. Divide participants into equal groups of about 2-8.
2. Place a grocery sack in front of each group on the floor.
3. Each participant must pick up the bag using only his/her teeth, while the only part of the body that can touch the floor is one's feet. Other group members can help in any way necessary, but also cannot touch the bag.
4. Once everyone in the group has attempted to lift the bag, cut two inches off the bag and have each member again try to lift the bag using only teeth.
5. Keep cutting the bag shorter and shorter while teammates cheer them on.

Materials: A large paper grocery bag and scissors for each group	**Setup**: None	**Group Size**: 6 or more, divided into groups of about 2 to 8

B17   Do Little, Gain Much!

Goal: Energizer	**Ages**: 5-Adult	**Time**: 10-15 minutes

Directions:

1. Prior to the beginning the session, put containers holding building materials on each table.
2. Explain that the materials are for them to fidget with as they listen throughout the session.

Variations:

⇒ Stress balls, markers and paper or clay can also be used.
⇒ From time to time the facilitator may want to draw attention to a product and ask what inspired its creation.

Materials: Blocks, Legos, Tinker Toys (should be in containers)	**Setup**: Tables	**Group Size**: 5 or more participants

B18   It Does Move!

| **Goal**: Energizer | **Ages**: 5-Adult | **Time**: 5 minutes |

Directions:

1. Distribute materials to each participant.
2. Have the participants tie a thin piece of string (about 10 inches long) to the top of a paper clip.
3. Have the participants hold the string up with the string end in the fingers at about eye height. The paper clip should be dangling at the bottom end.
4. Tell each participant to keep their hands still and just concentrate on the paper clip and think about moving it to the left and right. (Everyone's paper clip should start swinging after about 30 seconds.)

| **Materials**: Paper clips, string | **Setup**: None | **Group Size**: Any size |

B19   Paper Expressions

| **Goal**: Energizer | **Ages**: 8-Adult | **Time**: 1 minute |

Directions:

1. Cover the tables in the room with paper. Put the crayons and markers in the center of the table.
2. Explain to participants that as the session goes on they might want to take notes, draw, doodle, etc. The crayons and markers are there for their drawing pleasure.
3. Invite participants to also record thoughts, expressions, or questions.
4. At the end of the session have tablemates share their drawings and/or statements.

| **Materials**: Paper tablecloths (sheets of butcher paper will work), crayons, markers | **Setup**: Tables and chairs | **Group Size**: 10-30 participants |

B20 Celebrating Each Other!

Goal: Energizer | **Ages**: 8-Adult | **Time**: 10-15 minutes

Directions:

1. Put stacks of old newspapers in the middle of the floor and have group members sit around them.
2. Tell the group each member must create a trophy for the person on his/her right.
3. The trophy must be made from the newspaper and reflect the positive qualities of the person it is for. Participants may tear or fold the newspaper in anyway they want to create the trophy.
4. After trophies have been created, hold an award ceremony. One participant at a time presents their trophy and explains why it is being presented.

Materials: A large stack of newspapers | **Setup**: None | **Group Size**: 4-20 participants

B21   Take Your Best Shot

Goal: Energizer | **Ages**: 6-Adult | **Time**: 10 minutes

Directions:

1. Direct participants to select an emotion and then act out the feeling when dribbling the ball and shooting at the basket.
2. Allow the rest of the participants to guess the emotion. The one that guesses the emotion will be the next one to "dribble" their emotion.

Materials: Basketball, basketball hoop or bushel basket | **Setup**: Large open area | **Group Size**: 4 or more participants

B22   Imagine This!

| **Goal**: Energizer | **Ages**: 6-Adult | **Time**: 10 minutes |

Directions:

1. Ask participants to imagine that they are one of the following: bug, bird, vehicle, or a circus performer.
2. Give each participant two minutes to come up with a description about how they would view each of the following: strict parents, teachers who give too much homework, and the current state of the environment.
3. Have several participants, speaking from the perspective of their imagined persona, describe their reactions to one or more of the given situations.

Variations:

⇒ Select creative alternatives to the objects or situations listed in 1 and 2 above.

| **Materials**: None | **Setup**: None | **Group Size**: Any size |

B23 Together Wherever We Go!

| **Goal**: Energizer | **Ages**: 5-Adult | **Time**: 10 minutes |

Directions:

1. Tell the group to break into pairs and that each pair must hold onto the rope, no matter what the activity.
2. Give each pair a length of rope and tell them to not let go.
3. Once the partners are "attached," give them various tasks, such as: running an obstacle course, sit-ups, shooting a ball in baskets, jumping rope, twirling a hula-hoop.
4. Discussion question: In what ways did having a partner make it easier or harder for you?

Variations:

⇒ Also attach the legs of each pair.

| **Materials**: A two-foot length of rope for each pair, balls, baskets, extra rope, hula hoops, etc. | **Setup**: Open space | **Group Size**: 6 or more, divided into pairs |

B24 I Know a Yarn About You

| **Goal**: Energizer | **Ages**: 8-Adult | **Time**: 10-15 minutes |

Directions:

1. Give participants index cards and have each write one thing they would like others to know about them.
2. Divide the participants into groups of 8-10 and form circles.
3. Give each group a ball of yarn.
4. Explain to the group they are going to attach their card to the yarn using tape and tell the group what is on the tag when they receive the ball of yarn.
5. Start the activity and make sure everyone gets the ball of yarn.

| **Materials**: Ball of yarn for each group, index cards, tape | **Setup**: None | **Group Size**: Any size, divided into groups of about 8-10 |

B25   It's Bumper Car Time!

| **Goal**: Energizer | **Ages**: 5-Adult | **Time**: 5-8 minutes |

Directions:

1. Ask, "How may of you have ever ridden a bumper car?"
2. Invite participants to pretend that they are bumper cars. Think about how often you hear, "Guess who I bumped into today?"
3. The rules are:
⇒ When the music begins, everyone should begin "driving around." When you hear a whistle, you should move into "collision." The number in each group will depend on whistle toots. If you hear three toots there need to be three people in a group and so forth.
⇒ When in this "collision," you should introduce yourself by name and tell something interesting about yourself.
⇒ When you hear one toot you should begin "driving again!"
⇒ Each time you "collide" you should be with different people.
4. Start your engines! Toot!

| **Materials**: Music, whistle | **Setup**: None | **Group Size**: Any size |

B26　　　We're Alike

Goal: Energizer	**Ages**: 5-Adult	**Time**: 5 minutes

Directions:

1. In this activity, people pair up by ways they're alike.
2. Ask all participants to stand.
3. As the music starts, they walk around the room introducing themselves. Explain to the group they will have a chance to meet people again.
4. Tell them you'll call out a characteristic or similarity a person might have and they should quickly find another person with that like or characteristic. For example, if favorite color is called out you should find a participant or small group that likes your favorite color. Then talk to them about something interesting about the characteristic for a few moments. If you cannot find a person or group with your favorite choice, join a person or group anyway!
5. Begin the activity and call out characteristics or similarities you notice, such as: similar height, favorite type of drink, favorite animal, favorite pizza topping, favorite fast food place, favorite vacation spot, favorite type of music, favorite time of day.

Materials: Upbeat music	**Setup**: Open space	**Group Size**: Any size

Section C

Communication

C 1   The Me Cube

Goal: Communication	**Ages**: 8-Adult	**Time**: 10 minutes

Directions:

1. Have each participant construct a cube out of the material provided by cutting the paper in half length-wise and then dividing and folding each strip into thirds. Tape the sides together to form a cube shape.
2. After the cube is made, have participants decorate each of the six sides with words or pictures that describe their lives.
3. In groups of 4-6, discuss the personal meaning of the various sides of the cubes.

Materials: Paper (heavy), tape, old magazines, markers, scissors	**Setup**: Large area with tables	**Group Size**: Any size, divided into groups of 4-6

C 2   My Shadow Knows

Goal: Communication	**Ages**: 8-Adult	**Time**: 20-30 minutes

Directions:

1. Divide the participants into pairs.
2. Tell each participant in the pair to take turns making a silhouette of themselves:
    ⇒ Each can lie down on the newspaper while their partner traces around their body, or
    ⇒ Use a light to cast a shadow while the partner traces the silhouette.
3. Cut the silhouettes from the newspaper using the scissors.
4. Tell participants to cut out pictures from magazines/newspapers and glue these on the silhouette to make a collage.
5. The collage should illustrate what each participant is like, or values; things each may think or feel.
6. Hang the collages up using the tape.
7. In the larger group, each participant should share a few values they hold as illustrated by the collage.

Variations:

⇒ Let the participants make a collage about someone else they value/respect.

Materials: Light projector, newspaper, markers, magazines, scissors, glue, tape	**Setup**: Large open area	**Group Size**: Groups of less than 15, divided into pairs

C3　Pictures in My Mind

Goal: Communication	Ages: 8-Adult	Time: 10 minutes

Directions:

1. Divide participants into groups of 3-4.
2. Pass out paper and markers to each group.
3. Tell participants to divide their paper into four parts. They can draw lines or make two even folds in the paper.
4. Have each participant draw a symbol or slogan which represents their place of work or school from each of the following categories: banner, plant, car, comic strip character; and a reason why the symbol or slogan fits their setting.
5. After 5 minutes have the participants share their symbols or slogans in the whole group.
6. As a large group, share the most humorous and meaningful.

Variations:

⇒　Substitute any other symbols or settings appropriate to the reason for the group meeting.

Materials: Paper, markers	Setup: Drawing surfaces	Group Size: No more than 20, divided into groups of 3-4

C4　Oh, the Hats We Wear!

Goal: Communication	Ages: 11-Adult	Time: 15-20 minutes

Directions:

1. Divide participants into small groups of 3 or 4 and give each group a set of materials.
2. Tell each group to determine one role they all have in common and discuss how each feels about that role. (Allow a few minutes for their discussion.)
3. Each group must then create a hat which illustrates the common role. Use the colored strips to decorate the hats and write messages. Make sure every member contributes in some way (allow no more than 10 minutes for this activity).
4. Each group will introduce itself to the other groups by circulating and explaining their hats and common roles.

Variations:

⇒　Participants can use the leftover hat bands to list other roles each has as an individual (i.e., chauffeur, consumer, daughter, parent) and share them with the group.

Materials: Each group will need the following: 3 8½" x 11" sheets of paper, heavy weight paper strips of various colors (26" long, 4" wide), markers, glue bottle or stick, tape or stapler, scissors	Setup: None	Group Size: Any size, divided into groups of 3-4

C 5   I f I W e r e a T r e e

Goal: Communication	**Ages**: 12-Adult	**Time**: 15 minutes

Directions:

1. Tell the participants to draw a tree that represents their life up until now. For example, are you out on a limb or at the bottom?
2. Place a bird somewhere in the tree that shows where you are in life.
3. Draw the ground in a color that shows your feelings in childhood.
4. Draw objects around the tree that represent your family and friends.
5. Draw things in the background that represent good memories, or things you'd rather forget.
6. Ask volunteers to share the symbolism in their drawings.

Variations:

⇒   Instead of a tree, use flowers and put an insect on the flower.

Materials: Paper, pencils, markers, crayons	**Setup**: Room with desks	**Group Size**: Any size

C 6   S o u n d s o f t h e P a s t

Goal: Communication	**Ages**: 6-Adult	**Time**: 10 minutes

Directions:

1. Before the activity begins, record all types of sounds using a tape player or purchase a sound effects CD and select some appropriate sounds.
2. Give each participant a pencil and a piece of paper. As you play the sounds for the group, have each write down and share memories of places the sounds evoke.
3. Ask participants to explain if any of the sounds create negative feelings.
4. Discuss how sounds in the environment can set a mood. What changes of sound can participants suggest to promote more positive moods?

Materials: Tape recorder or CD player, blank cassette tape or sound effects CD, paper, pencils	**Setup**: None	**Group Size**: Any size

C7   It's All in My Head

Goal: Communication	**Ages**: 12-Adult	**Time**: 10-15 minutes

Directions:

1. Pass out a sheet of paper to each participant.
2. Refer to the illustration (C7) and ask each participant to draw the shape of his/her head on the sheet of paper (full-sized; hair and other details should also be drawn in as appropriate.
3. Inside the head, each participant should write or draw items that represent each of the following categories: things that make you happy, things that make you sad, hobbies you enjoy, things you are afraid of, and something you hope for your future.
4. Have each participant tape the piece of paper to their clothing with the head showing.
5. Have each participant walk around the room for a few minutes with a marker. If a participant sees something represented on another participant's head that he/she had represented on his/her own head, circle the representation on the other participant's head.
6. After this time, make a list of items held in common on chart paper and tally the occurrence of each item.

Variations:

⇒   When a participant sees an item similar to his/her own, have him/her introduce him/herself to the other participant, and continue on to the next person.
⇒   This activity can also be used as a "Starter."

Materials: Paper, tape, markers, Illustration, chart paper	**Setup**: Large enough room so participants can walk around	**Group Size**: 30 or fewer participants

---

Illustration C7: It's All in My Head

1.   Things that make you happy
2.   Things that make you sad
3.   Hobbies you enjoy
4.   Things you are afraid of
5.   What you think about the future

C8   Making My Own Cup

Goal: Communication	**Ages**: 8-Adult	**Time**: 15 minutes

Directions:

Note: The facilitator is advised to practice making the cup prior to using this activity.

1. Instruct participants that they will be making a cup using the Japanese paper folding technique of Origami.
2. Read the "Making My Own Cup" handout (see illustration C8) quickly without stopping. (Ask that all questions or comments be held until the end.)
3. Give each participant a sheet of paper and instruct them to make the cup.
4. If they have difficulty, ask them why. Answers might be:
   - a. no time to clarify.
   - b. directions given too quickly.
   - c. no visuals.
   - d. no step-by-step directions.
5. Give each participant a copy of illustration C8. Again, read the handout. Allow questions and instruct each participant to make the cup again. This time clarify questions and answers by using visuals and questions. The task should proceed more smoothly.
6. Discuss with the group the benefits of communication and instructions.

Variations:

⇒   Any type of paper construction can be used (e.g., airplane).

⇒   Pass out a snack or candy to be placed in each cup as a reward.

Materials: One sheet of paper (8 ½"x 11") and one instruction page (Illustration C8: Making My Own Cup) per participant	**Setup**: None	**Group Size**: Any size

Illustration C8: Making My Own Cup

1. Fold up the bottom half so corners meet at top.

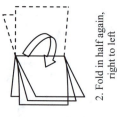

2. Fold in half again, right to left

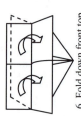

3. Unfold from left to right

4. Fold right corner to the center

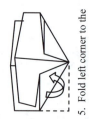

5. Fold left corner to the corner

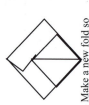

6. Fold down front top flap

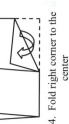

7. Fold down back flap

8. Pull the front and back apart & rotate cup 90 degrees to the right

9. Make a new fold so the cup looks like this

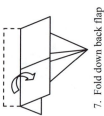

10. Fold down front top flap & crease it

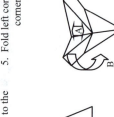

11. Fold down the top back flap

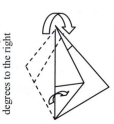

12. Pull front & back apart gently to make the cup

C 9 It's a Match!

| Goal: Communication | Ages: 10-Adult | Time: 10-15 minutes |

Directions:

1. Preparation: All puzzles should be created before the session. Images, themes, goals, etc. can be glued on the cardboard. All like puzzle pieces should have the same border so they will be easy to find. Cut each puzzle into 4 pieces. The puzzle is simply a sorting technique.
2. As participants arrive before the session begins, give each a puzzle piece from a large box .
3. Give a brief welcome and orientation to the session by telling participants they are to find three other participants in the room who have complementing puzzle pieces so that the 4 participants will have a complete puzzle.
4. Tell participants to walk around the room comparing their puzzle pieces with the others. When they find a matching piece, have each introduce themselves and work as a team to find the participants with the rest of the puzzle. All groups will end up with 4 participants. (If a group is short a person or persons, they should look in the large puzzle box for their missing pieces).
5. The groups should then find a place to work and put all the pieces of the puzzle together.
6. When groups have put their pieces together, distribute to each group markers, glue, tape, newsprint, and scissors.
7. Groups should construct and glue their picture to the top of the newsprint.
8. Groups should then brainstorm some good communication or relationship skills demonstrated in the picture and list each below the picture using the markers.
9. Have each group tape the newsprint to a wall and share with the entire group.

Variations:

⇒ By using different puzzle themes, this activity can be adapted to virtually any group purpose. Relationship groups could have pictures of families; peer helper groups could show various communication skills such as listening, etc.

| Materials: For each group: A 4 piece puzzle (paste a newsprint or magazine picture illustrating communication skills to a piece of tag board, then cut the puzzle into 4 variously sized and shaped pieces), newsprint, markers, glue, tape | Setup: Large room with tables and chairs or large space | Group Size: Any size |

C 10 A Window's View

| Goal: Communication | Ages: 10-Adult | Time: 10 minutes |

Directions:

1. Divide the participants into groups of four or more.
2. Ask each member of the group to take turns answering the question "If this window (door, carpet, etc.) could talk, what would it say about our group?"
3. Have each group do more than one round.
4. Allow group members to ask questions about the answers given.

Variations:

⇒ Have the group replace the word "window" with other objects that the group comes in contact with frequently.

| Materials: None | Setup: None | Group Size: Any size, divided into groups of 4 or more |

C 11   CEO for a Day

| **Goal**: Communication | **Ages**: 12-Adult | **Time**: 10-15 minutes |

Directions:

1. Divide participants into groups of about 5.
2. Ask the participants to think about people who have influenced them in their lives.
3. Tell each participant that they are going to be CEOs for a day and need to have a board meeting.
4. They are to complete the "CEO for a Day" worksheet provided and list people who have influenced them and why. What types of decisions could they help the participant make?
5. After the participants have completed the worksheet, have them share their board of directors with the group.

| **Materials**: Pencils, markers, "CEO for a Day" worksheet (see illustration C11) | **Setup**: Tables | **Group Size**: Any size, divided into groups of about 5 |

Illustration C11: CEO for a Day

Board of Directors: People Who Influence You and How

1. _____

2. _____

3. _____

4. _____

5. _____

What type of decisions does your board have to make?

48

C12　　　What Is It?

| **Goal**: Communication | **Ages**: 8-Adult | **Time**: 5-10 minutes |

Directions:

1. Divide participants into groups of 4 to 10.
2. Select two group participants to identify a single object in the room.
3. In order for them to get the group to guess what the object is, these participants must carry on a conversation about the object without directly saying what it is.
4. The group should be listening during the conversation and attempting to guess the mystery object.

| **Materials**: None | **Setup**: None | **Group Size**: 4 or more, divided into groups of 4-10 |

C13　　　My "Feelings" Bank

| **Goal**: Communication | **Ages**: 8-Adult | **Time**: Any time during class |

Directions:

1. Before the session begins, decorate the cans using whatever decorative material is available.
2. Explain to participants that these cans can hold feelings that may occur during the session as well as new things they've learned.
3. Throughout the session, participants can write on the slips of paper provided and place these thoughts and feelings in their can.

Note: This is a personal bank and the slips of paper will only be seen by the participants.

| **Materials**: A decorated can for each participant, small slips of paper, pencils | **Setup**: None | **Group Size**: Any size |

C14   Across the River

| **Goal**: Communication | **Ages**: 6-Adult | **Time**: 5-10 minutes |

Directions:

1. At the start of the ladder, participants will write, "I will…" and their specific goal.
2. On each rung of the ladder, have participants write the steps needed to reach the goal.
3. On each side of the ladder, place a support, resource, or strategy that will be needed to complete each step.
4. Ask participants to pair up and share their goal ladder with their partner.

Facilitator note: Use this activity in any session focused on problem solving or behavior change. Participants need to think about specific steps needed to meet a goal.

| **Materials**: 1 "Across the River" worksheet (see the illustration C14) and pen per participant | **Setup**: None | **Group Size**: Any size |

Illustration C14: Across the River

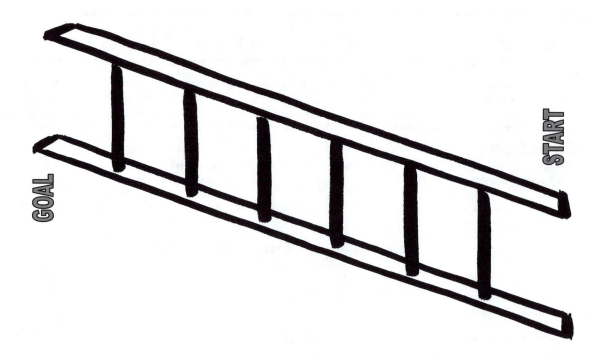

GOAL

START

C15 Trim the Tree with Emotions

| **Goal**: Communication | **Ages**: 5-Adult | **Time**: 10 minutes |

Directions:

1. Put the outline of a large paper tree on the board.
2. Ask each participant to cut out an ornament from the paper in any shape or form desired and decorate the ornament in a way which shows an emotion each has felt over the past few days.
3. When completed, have each participant tape the ornament to the tree and discuss the emotion they chose.

Variations:

⇒ At the end of the session, have participants identify emotions from the tree that were experienced during the session.
⇒ Look at the emotions displayed on the tree and have participants identify emotions that have not been listed.

| **Materials**: Cut out ornaments (one for each participant; see Illustration C15), tape, colored markers, scissors, paper | **Setup**: None | **Group Size**: 10-50 participants |

Illustration C15: Trim the Tree with Emotions

C16　Hanging Anger Out to Dry

Goal: Communication	**Ages**: 12-Adult	**Time**: 15 minutes

Directions:

1. Before the activity begins, cut out a paper shirt for each person participating. Paper shirts can be made out of any large paper product, such as table covering or newsprint.
2. Hang a clothesline across the room with clothespins on it.
3. Divide participants into groups of about four and give each group a paper shirt, paint and markers.
4. Ask each group to think about and discuss ways that bodies react to anger.
5. Have each group write or draw on the shirts the various bodily reactions to anger.
6. When finished, each group should hang their shirts on the clothesline to "dry."
7. As a large group, discuss how body signals can help us to control (dry) the anger.

Variations:

⇒　Rather than anger, select another emotion that may be the focus of the group (e.g., depression, anxiety, happiness, stress).

Materials: Paper shirts, body paint, markers, clothes pins, clothesline	**Setup**: Large room	**Group Size**: Any size, divided into groups of about 4

C17　An Emotional Puppet Show

Goal: Communication	**Ages**: 6-Adult	**Time**: 15 minutes

Directions:

1. Instruct the participants to construct a puppet from a paper lunch bag, decorated as desired..
2. This puppet will display an emotion of the puppet maker's choice (e.g., joy, sorrow, anger). Participants should strive to present a diverse range of emotions.
3. After each participant has created a puppet, have each write the types of things that would make a person feel that emotion on the back of the paper lunch bag.
4. Divide participants into groups of 3-6 and have each group design a puppet show expressing the puppets' emotions as part of the story line.
5. As a group discuss which emotions would be difficult to express and why.

Materials: Paper lunch bags, color markers, string, ribbon, construction paper, scissors, glue	**Setup**: None	**Group Size**: Any size

C18   What Is in My Heart?

Goal: Communication	**Ages**: 8-Adult	**Time**: 10 minutes

Directions:

Background: Explain that the things we keep hidden inside on a daily basis are hurts, pain, and anger. This activity gives people the opportunity to express their pain and to encourage sharing the good things in their hearts with others.

1. Distribute paper bags with materials to each member of the group. Tell them that the small balloon represents their heart and all the pain, hurt, and anger that can be folded inside it.
2. Instruct participants to cut slips of paper that are small enough to fit in the small balloon and write down all their hurts and anger. Then put these pieces of paper in the balloon.
3. Tie the balloon closed with the ribbon. Do not blow up the balloon. (The papers are not to be shared with anyone.)
4. Give each participant a large balloon and have each put the small balloon inside the large balloon. Tell each participant to blow up the large balloon and tie it shut.
5. Tell each participant to write on the outside how they present themselves to others so others will not see the things that are hidden on the inside (i.e., look confident, happy).
6. Ask the participants to discuss what is written on the outside of their balloons. Ask participants to share one thing that is written inside their balloon.
7. After the group has finished, have each person pop their balloon as a way of getting rid of the anger or pain.
8. After the balloons are popped, the hearts should remain (the smaller balloons).
9. Challenge the group to share what's in their "heart" during the week.

Materials: Each participant will need a small bag with the following materials: pins, paper, markers, scissors, thin pieces of ribbon, one balloon (small, not inflated), one large balloon.	**Setup**: None	**Group Size**: 10 to 15 participants

---

C19   Cookie Design Party

Goal: Communication	**Ages**: 6-Adult	**Time**: 15 minutes

Directions:

1. Put all the cookie supplies in the center of each table.
2. Tell each participant to decorate a cookie.
3. When finished, have participants share how the cookie represents their feelings at the present time.
4. Ask participants to wrap up the cookie and give it to someone they trust. Tell participants to tell interested persons what the cookie means and why they were chosen to receive it.
5. Discuss: Was it difficult to identify someone to give your cookie to? What makes people trustworthy?

Materials: Pre-made cookies, frosting (different colors), cookie decorating supplies, plastic knife, plastic wrap, plastic gloves	**Setup**: Tables	**Group Size**: Any size

C20 Friendship Banner

Goal: Communication	**Ages**: 6-Adult	**Time**: 20 minutes

Directions:

1. Begin a short discussion on the meaning of friendship. Ask each group to make a friendship banner with symbols which represent the following:
   - a. What you look for in a friend.
   - b. Something that makes you a good friend.
   - c. How you feel when people are friendly to you.
2. Display the banners on the wall.

Materials: For each group provide 1 large piece of paper for a banner, markers, and tape	**Setup**: Tables and wall space	**Group Size**: Any size, divided into groups of about 4

C21 The Buildings of My Life

Goal: Communication	**Ages**: 12-Adult	**Time**: 10 minutes

Directions:

1. Instruct participants to fold their papers into four equal parts.
2. In each quadrant, have participants draw a house, building or surroundings, which represent their feelings about 4 different periods of their lives (e.g., infancy, early childhood, elementary school, teen age years, living alone with mom, etc.).
3. Use colors to represent the feelings about that time.
4. When finished, have participants volunteer to share their drawings and feelings.

Materials: Paper, markers	**Setup**: Tables	**Group Size**: Any size

C22   How Life Changes

Goal: Communication | **Ages**: 8-Adult | **Time**: 10 minutes

Directions:

1. Have each participant draw a line across the paper.
2. Explain that this line represents their life from the beginning (on the left) to now (on the right).
3. Have participants place dots on the line where their life changed in some way.
4. Under each dot, put the age when the event occurred and on top of the dot put the event.
5. Have participants volunteer to share some times when their life changed, how they felt at the time, and how they feel about the events now.

Materials: Paper, pencils | **Setup**: A writing surface | **Group Size**: Any size

---

C23   Pass the Pillow

Goal: Communication | **Ages**: 6-Adult | **Time**: 10 minutes

Directions:

1. Tell participants that the pillow in this activity symbolizes safety and security.
2. Have participants sit in a circle.
3. Explain to participants that they will pass the pillow from person to person, each person sharing something about themselves.
4. When everyone has had a turn, take the pillow back and ask if anyone has thought of something they would like to add. Continue until it is time to change the activity.

Variations:

⇒ Explain to participants that the pillow is available anytime during the session when they have something to share. Thus, the pillow can be used to enforce the common group rule that only one participant should talk at a time.

Materials: One small pillow | **Setup**: None | **Group Size**: 6-12

C24   Me, Myself, and I

Goal: Communication	**Ages**: 7-Adult	**Time**: 10-12 minutes (about 30 seconds per participant)

Directions:

1. Explain that participants will discover things about themselves and possibly share these insights with the group.
2. Give each participant the 3 "feeling cards" and a pencil. Have each participant fill in the card for each of the following 3 sentences:
   a. "I am feeling ___."
   b. "I don't like to feel____ because ____."
   c. "I like to feel ____ because ____."
3. Give ample time to fill in sentences on the cards. When ready, have participants read their sentences to the group. Introduce the "Pass" rule (i.e., OK not to share). The facilitator may consider modeling by going first.
4. Ask if it was easy or hard to fill in sentences and why. Talk about the advantages and disadvantages of telling others about yourself in a group.

Variations:

⇒   Break into small groups for sharing.
⇒   Consider other sentences such as: "I often feel ___ because____;" "I am not ____ ;" "Right now in this group I feel ___."
⇒   For younger ages, eliminate writing and ask one question at a time.

Materials: Feelings cards (see illustration C24), paper and pencil for each, flip chart	**Setup**: Horseshoe seating and writing surface	**Group Size**: Any size (best results with smaller groups)

Illustration C24: Feeling Cards

Feeling Card #1:

I am feeling _____.

Feeling Card #2:

I don't like to feel _____

because _____.

Feeling Card #3:

I like to feel _____

because _____.

C25   Filling Your Plate

Goal: Communication	**Ages**: 8-Adult	**Time**: 3-5 minutes each time

Directions:

1. Give each participant a paper plate.
2. Tell the participants to draw lines to divide the plate into the number of topics to be discussed that day. This must be determined ahead of time by the facilitator.
3. Tell participants that during the session, they will hear information or gain insights from certain topics.
4. After hearing information on the topic at some point during the session, participants should write 3 words which describe their reactions to the topic.
5. After the discussion ends, ask participants to share reactions with the group.

Materials: One 6" paper plate for each participant, markers	**Setup**: None	**Group Size**: 4 or more participants

C26   Avoiding Life's Traps

Goal: Communication	**Ages**: 10-Adult	**Time**: 10 minutes

Directions:

1. Divide the participants into groups of about 8.
2. Ask the question "What gets in the way of you being the best you can be?"
3. Ask each group to list "traps" that keep them from communicating with family, friends, teachers, and so on (such as dishonesty, procrastination, prejudice).
4. Have the group discuss any ideas that are helpful in avoiding these traps.
5. Have each group make a banner representing all the ideas that help avoid being caught in a trap.

Materials: Large sheets of paper, crayons, markers	**Setup**: Large area for groups	**Group Size**: Any size, divided into groups of about 8

C27 What Does Your Wheel Look Like?

| **Goal**: Communication | **Ages**: 12-Adult | **Time**: 15 minutes |

Directions:

1. Divide the participants into groups of about 8.
2. Tell the participants they have $500 to spend. This money is very, very special. It will only buy things like health, love, adventure, beauty, wisdom, and friendship.
3. Pass out the "wheel" worksheets (see Illustration C27), newsprint, and markers.
4. Have participants fill out the worksheets by delegating a portion of their money to the categories and then share their information with the group. Each group should select a recorder and summarize the group information from the worksheets.

Variations:

⇒ Participants can create additional dividers in the wheel.
⇒ Give each participant $500 in play money at the beginning of the activity.

| **Materials**: Markers and newsprint for each group, a worksheet (see illustration C27) for each participant | **Setup**: None | **Group Size**: Any size, divided into groups of about 8 |

Illustration C27: What Does Your Wheel Look Like?

C28 You Can't Worm Out of It

Goal: Communication	**Ages**: 5-Adult	**Time**: 3-5 minutes

Directions:

1. Organize participants into groups of 3-4.
2. Put a bowl of gummy worms in the middle of each table and give each person a napkin.
3. Tell each participant they have to think of an event that has happened to them that has caused them discomfort. (They can't worm out of not answering, but they will also be rewarded for their answer.)
4. Have participants share their event with the group. After they have shared, they should reward themselves by taking a gummy worm.
5. Continue around the table as time allows.

Materials: Napkins, bowls with gummy worms	**Setup**: Room with tables	**Group Size**: 6-40 participants, divided into teams of 3-4

C29 Gripe! Gripe! Gripe!

Goal: Communication	**Ages**: 5-Adult	**Time**: 5-10 minutes

Directions:

1. Divide the participants into groups of 5-6 and have the groups sit in a circle.
2. Everyone gets a turn to say what angers, annoys, or frustrates them.
3. Participants are to say who was involved, what was done about the problem, and if the situation was resolved.

Variations:

⇒ With young children, an anger puppet or a magic microphone (a wooden dowel with two feet of yarn attached) adds fun to this activity.

Materials: None	**Setup**: None	**Group Size**: Any size, divided into groups of 5-6 participants

C30   Be a Good Egg!

Goal: Communication	**Ages**: 6-Adult	**Time**: None

Directions:

1. Distribute one "Be a Good Egg" worksheet, crayons, and scissors to each participant.
2. Have each participant cut out, decorate, and write ways to be good friends (or some other topic that is the group's focus) on their eggs.
3. After everyone is finished, hang the decorated eggs around the room as each participant shares one or two of their ideas.

Materials: For each participant, provide one "Be a Good Egg" worksheet (see Illustration C30), scissors, crayons, tape	**Setup**: None	**Group Size**: 10-30 participants

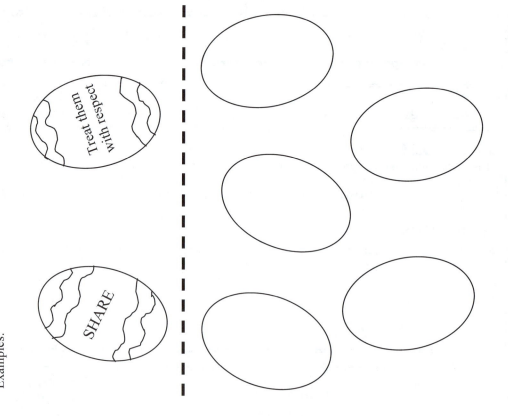

Illustration C30: Be a Good Egg

Examples:

Treat them with respect

SHARE

C31   S o u n d   t h e   A l a r m

Goal: Communication	**Ages**: 12-Adult	**Time**: 5-10 minutes

Directions:

1. Divide the participants into groups of about 6.
2. Write personal signals of stress on the "Sound the Alarm" worksheet.
3. Have the groups discuss warning signals of stress and list these on the group's sheet of paper.
4. As an entire group, share strategies for dealing with stress.

Variations:

⇒   Anger or another emotion can be the focus instead of stress.

Materials: One "Sound the Alarm" worksheet per participant (see Illustration C31), note paper, markers, and tape for each group	**Setup**: None	**Group Size**: Any size, divided into groups of about 6

Illustration C31: Sound the Alarm

STRESS

Directions: Write personal signs of stress in the space below.

YOUR EMOTIONS	YOUR BODY
SPIRIT	RELATIONSHIPS
INTERNAL SIGNS	WORK/SCHOOL

C32   It's Compliment Time!

Goal: Communication	Ages: 8-Adult	Time: 15-20 minutes

Directions:

1. Divide the participants into groups of 3-4.
2. Ask each group member to list three compliments they could give someone on three separate index cards.
3. Then have participants list three "put downs" they've heard recently on the other three index cards.
4. Put the compliments and put downs into the group bag.
5. Pull one card at a time from the bag and read it aloud.
6. As a group, decide whether each statement is a compliment or a put down.
7. If it is a put down, the group should determine how such a statement might make someone feel and how, as someone who witnessed the put down, you might be able to help the situation.

Materials: Bag, markers, scissors, 6 index cards per participant	Setup: None	Group Size: Any size, divided into groups of 3-4

C33   That Is My Hat!

Goal: Communication	Ages: 5-Adult	Time: 5-10 minutes

Directions:

1. Ask participants to sit in a circle.
2. Select one member from the group and ask them to choose the hat in the pile that best represents how they are feeling right now.
3. Discuss the feeling and the circumstances creating the feeling. Put the hat back in the center.
4. In turn, allow each person in the group to select a hat. After each hat is selected, participants should share the feeling and circumstances.

Variations:

⇒ At the end, participants could design a hat on paper that best represents them.
⇒ Additional queries could be:
    ⇒ How do you feel when you're with this group?
    ⇒ How do you feel when you're with your family?
    ⇒ How do you feel when you're alone, at work, or at school?

Materials: A large pile of different hats	Setup: Area where people can sit in circles	Group Size: 2-25 participants

C34   If I Could Choose a Picture

| **Goal**: Communication | **Ages**: 8-Adult | **Time**: 10-15 minutes |

Directions:

1. Before the session begins, cut out the designs in the illustration (C34) and place all the designs inside an envelope for each person (all designs in each envelope).
2. Divide the participants into groups of about 6 and give each participant an envelope with the cut out pictures from the resource sheet.
3. Tell each participant to select one design which they feel best describes them. If none of the pictures fit, have participants draw their own picture on the back of a design. Give them a few minutes to make their selections.
4. Have group members share their selected pictures with the group and discuss why they believe the design is like them.

| *Materials:* Envelopes with cut out pictures (see Illustration C34; one per participant), markers, scissors | **Setup**: None | **Group Size**: Any size, divided into groups of about 6 |

Illustration C34: If I Could Choose a Picture

CLOUDS

MOUNTAINS

SUN

RAINBOW

RAIN

OCEAN

STAR

TREE

FLOWERS

63

C35　　My Parts of the Puzzle

| **Goal**: Communication | **Ages**: 8-Adult | **Time**: 10 minutes |

Directions:
1. Explain that the group will be putting a puzzle together.
2. Pass out the materials to each participant.
3. Have the participants cut the piece of construction paper into at least eight pieces.
4. Ask the participants to write facets of their life on the eight pieces (e.g., home, school, weekends, private time, hopes, dreams, friends, hobbies).
5. Have the participants write a few words of description on each piece.
6. What part would you change if any? Write how you would change that part of your life on the back of the puzzle.

| **Materials**: Construction paper, markers, scissors, envelopes | **Setup**: Tables | **Group Size**: Any size |

C36　　　This Is Me!

| **Goal**: Communication | **Ages**: 5-Adult | **Time**: 30 minutes |

Directions:
1. Several days before this activity, have participants collect (from magazines, newspapers, etc.) pictures which are representative of them. Tell participants to wear comfortable clothing for the activity day.
2. On the day of the activity, have participants work in pairs. Give each pair large sheets of newspaper and markers.
3. Have one participant lay down on the paper while the other traces around their body outline. Then have the other partner do the same.
4. Each person should then cut around the outline and put pictures which represent themselves on their silhouette.
5. Go around the room and have everyone share their figures.

| **Materials**: Large sheets of newspaper, markers, magazines, glue, scissors, pictures which represent the students | **Setup**: Large area | **Group Size**: Any size |

C37 Oh, the Things That Are in a Purse

| **Goal**: Communication | **Ages**: 8-Adult | **Time**: 10 minutes |

Directions:

1. Place a group of articles such as those suggested in the materials list on the table.
2. Have each participant pick up an article without looking at the item.
3. Tell the groups they are to take a few minutes to imagine that they are that item. (I am a pencil. I am made of wood, metal, and rubber. I can erase all of my mistakes, etc.)
4. Each participant should then take a turn describing how the item is like them.

| **Materials**: Lipstick, pencil, wallet, paperclip, stamps, coins, and other common objects | **Setup**: Desks or tables for people to sit around | **Group Size**: Any size, divided into groups of about 4 |

C38   Excuse the Interruption

| **Goal**: Communication | **Ages**: 8-Adult | **Time**: 10-15 minutes |

Directions:

1. Stories, tales, skits, and exaggerations often make a huge impact when sharing ideas.
2. Divide the large group into smaller groups of about 4 participants.
3. Allow 4-5 minutes for participants in each group to think of and share how interruptions can and have ruined their day.
4. Have each group act out a situation or tell a story where an interruption has ruined the day.

Variations:

⇒   Have individuals discuss the situation, rather than act it out.

| **Materials**: 1 chair for each participant (optional) | **Setup**: Room where small groups of 4 can sit in a circle | **Group Size**: Any number of participants, divided into groups of about 4 |

C39   You Rule!

| **Goal**: Communication | **Ages**: 12-Adult | **Time**: 20-25 minutes |

Directions:

1. Divide participants into groups of 4-6 and distribute the newsprint, markers, and one "land" card to each group. Tell each group to notice the name of the land it has been transported to.
2. Tell participants to design a very basic government for their land (e.g., some laws should be designed for governing people, election of leaders, etc.).
3. Have each group record the laws and other information about its land on the newsprint.
4. Allow 10-15 minutes for the groups to implement the activity.
5. At the end of this time have each group hang their newsprint on the wall (using the masking tape) and explain the created government to the rest of the participants.

Variations:

⇒   Rather than composing rules of government, have each group compose rules for the treatment of group members when working on projects or interacting with one another.
⇒   This activity can also be used for Team Building.

| **Materials**: 1 "land" card (see Illustration C39 - be sure to use lands appropriate for the age group), sheet of newsprint and marker per team, one roll of masking tape | **Setup**: None | **Group Size**: Any size, divided into groups of 4-6 |

Illustration C39: Land Cards

MAGIC KINGDOM	NEVER-NEVER LAND	LAND OF MILK AND HONEY	SAME LAND	NOW LAND
All the fairytale characters live.	No one ever grows up.	Everyone has more than they will ever need.	Everyone is the same.	There is no past or future.
CANDY LAND	THE LAND OF OZ	TROPICAL PARADISE	LA LA LAND	YUK LAND
Everything in it is made of Candy.	Dorothy, Toto, Lion, Scarecrow, and Tin Man live.	Everyone has everything they need.	Nothing is what is seems to be.	Everything is rotten.

Section D

Team Building

D 1   You Can "Peak!"

| **Goal**: Team Building | **Ages**: 8-Adult | **Time**: 8 minutes |

Directions:

1. Before the activity, build a structure with the materials at a difficulty level appropriate for the participants' age. Hide the structure so the groups can't see it.
2. Divide participants into groups of about four.
3. Ask one member from each group to look at the structure for 10 seconds.
4. Have the member return to the group and tell, in words only, how to build the structure.
5. After one minute have a second member of each group "peek" at the structure.
6. Continue until teams successfully duplicate the structure or until each group member has peeked at the structure.
7. Discussion questions:
    a. How did each participant help the group to "peak?"
    b. How can teamwork help you in daily life?

| **Materials**: Building blocks (blocks, Legos, etc.) for each group | **Setup**: Tables or a large clear space | **Group Size**: 6 or more, divided into groups of about 4 |

D 2   It's Not Trash

| **Goal**: Team Building | **Ages**: 5-Adult | **Time**: 10 minutes |

Directions:

1. Divide participants into groups of 3-4.
2. Place all the items in the center of the table. Use different items for each table to make it more interesting.
3. Tell the group to create a "piece of art" as a group.
4. Have each group create a story about the artwork.
5. When the group has completed the artwork, allow time for an art display of the finished products and have each group share the story that goes with that piece of art.

| **Materials**: For each group: markers, scissors, glue, tape, any "garbage" item (paper towel rolls, egg cartons, foil, cans, yarn, paper, etc.) | **Setup**: None | **Group Size**: Any size, divided into groups of 3-4 |

D3   How High Can You Go?

| **Goal**: Team Building | **Ages**: 5-Adult | **Time**: 5-8 minutes |

Directions:

1. Give each group a stack of paper and nothing else.
2. Instruct the groups to build the highest structure they can using only paper.
3. Set the group goal of using at least five sheets of paper to build the structure.

Hint: There are many ways to build a paper tower but one of the best ways is to fold each piece of paper into three sections, open up the paper slightly and stack the sheets on top of each other. One can place horizontal sheets between the stacked sheets.

| **Materials**: Paper | **Setup**: None | **Group Size**: Any size, divided into groups of 3-5 |

D4   Cleaning Up

| **Goal**: Team Building | **Ages**: 8-Adult | **Time**: 15 minutes |

Directions:

1. Divide the participants into groups of 8-20.
2. Instruct each group to build a machine that will pick up paper scraps from the table.
3. One person from each group will pour the scraps of paper on the table.
4. Each group will use the materials on the table to design a machine to pick up the paper. The group will be given 10 minutes to design and build their machine.
5. The machine will be tested when the ten minutes are up.
6. To encourage competition, each group can be given 1 point for each piece of paper the machine collects.
7. As a large group, discuss the interpersonal/teamwork processes employed to get the job done.

| **Materials**: For each group: 10 drinking straws, masking tape, 2 pieces of cardboard, 4 paper clips, bag of scraps of paper (use self-sealing bags) | **Setup**: Tables for groups to use | **Group Size**: Any size, divided into groups of 8-20 |

D 5   I've Got It!

| **Goal**: Team Building | **Ages**: 8-Adult | **Time**: 5 minutes |

Directions:

1. Divide the participants into groups of 5-10.
2. Tell the whole group that they will be given 3 minutes to think silently about many possible (creative) ways the object in the center of the table can be used.
3. After the 3 minutes are up, have each group go around the table quickly, one by one, to share one idea.
4. Repeat this process until the group is out of ideas.
5. Discuss the creative processes necessary to get groups to "think outside the envelope."

| **Materials**: Any interesting objects (e.g., paper clip, pencil, etc.), one object per group. | **Setup**: Table or desk for each group to sit around | **Group Size**: Any size, divided into groups of 5-10 |

D 6   Let's Ski

| **Goal**: Team Building | **Ages**: 5-Adult | **Time**: 10 minutes |

Directions:

1. Instruct each group to build a "snow ski" by tying their (empty) shoes to the long board. Be sure that the shoes are spaced out equally along the boards. The shoes must all face the same way, and one shoe from each pair must be across from its mate.
2. Place the shoe skis at one end of the room and ask participants to put their feet in the shoes.
3. Give the group the task of moving as a unit to reach the other end successfully.
4. After the activity, discuss strategies employed to accomplish the task more smoothly.

Variations:

⇒ After an additional strategy session, ask participants to move across the room again by employing the new strategy.

| **Materials**: Each group needs: Two 2" x 4" x 6' boards, and strong string | **Setup**: Large room with plenty of open space | **Group Size**: Any size, divided into groups of 2-4 |

D7   A-Sailing We Will Go!

| **Goal**: Team Building | **Ages**: Adults or older teens | **Time**: 3-5 minutes |

Directions:

1. Organize the participants into groups of 8-10.
2. Ask for some participants who have done some sailing or boating (see "Variations" below for alternative activities) to come up front to demonstrate the activity.
3. Have the demonstrators decide on about 4 different physical movements involved in sailing that the groups could enact, complete with verbal expressions, and demonstrate these activities for the groups (e.g., hoist the sail, raise the anchor, swab the decks, hard to port, steady as she goes, etc.).
4. Explain that teamwork involves understanding everyone's role and responsibility, and this is evident in sailing (or other) competitions.
5. Tell participants in each group to arrange themselves as crew members might on a sailing vessel might, including the captain.
6. Have each captain take command of a group and lead them through the demonstrated activities.

Variations:

⇒   Rather than a sailing theme, choose another team activity with which participants may be more familiar, such as football, baseball, or even preparing a meal.

⇒   The entire group could engage in the activity at the same time with no demonstration – just tell them to role-play with other participants. Later, have participants discuss what made each adopt their role and responsibility and how their role contributed to team performance.

⇒   This activity can also be used as a "Starter."

| **Materials**: None | **Setup**: None | **Group Size**: Any size, divided into groups of 8-10 |

D8   I Can't Sail My Ship Alone

| **Goal**: Team Building | **Ages**: 6-Adult | **Time**: 10 minutes |

Directions:

1. Divide the participants into groups of 3 or 4.
2. Tell the groups to use the yardstick and tape to mark off an area that measures three feet long. Collect the rolls of masking tape and instruct the groups not to use masking tape to complete the following task.
3. Each group will then build a paper ship that will hold all the pennies. Only the materials supplied can be used (not the masking tape).
4. The group can only use the rubber bands to move the pennies forward. During the movement of the boat, no other materials can be used.
5. After teams reach the finish line, discuss the strategies used with the entire group.

Variations:

⇒   After an additional strategy session, have groups try the activity again.

| **Materials**: For each group: yard stick, 10 pennies, 20 rubber bands, 1 sheet of paper, masking tape | **Setup**: None | **Group Size**: Any size, divided into groups of 3 or 4 |

D9　A Building of Our Own

| **Goal**: Team Building | **Ages**: 8-Adult | **Time**: 15 minutes |

Directions:

1. Divide the participants into groups of 3-4 individuals.
2. Give each group a deck of cards. Have each group distribute the deck of cards approximately evenly to each member.
3. Instruct the group to construct a building of some sort to house their group.
4. Each participant must place their own cards and the group should use as many cards as possible.
5. Participants should offer suggestions as the building proceeds.
6. Tell the group to start and stop on your signal. Allow 10 minutes for the groups to complete a building. If the building collapses, have the groups start over again.
7. Ask the participants what difficulties each had.
8. Ask participants how the group's input helped or hindered concentration and performance.

| **Materials**: 1 deck of playing cards per group | **Setup**: Tables or desks | **Group Size**: Any size, divided into groups of 3-4 |

D10　Towel Relay

| **Goal**: Team Building | **Ages**: 6-Adult | **Time**: 10 minutes |

Directions:

1. Divide participants into even-numbered groups of approximately 10 and have each participant select a partner from among their teammates.
2. Distribute towels and balls to each group (1 towel for each pair and 1 ball per team).
3. Tell each group to spread out and arrange themselves so that each pair is in a straight line.
4. Each partner should grasp an end of the towel. Allow each pair of the group to practice tossing the ball up so the next pair in the line can catch it with their towel.
5. Have participants from each group then line up and toss the ball from towel to towel all the way up the line and back in practice for the competition.
6. Groups can compete to see which group can pass the ball, using towels, from one end of the line to the other and back the fastest without dropping the ball. If the ball is dropped, the group must start at the beginning again.
7. Discuss the factors that lead to successful performance and what may be needed to improve future performance.

Variations:

⇒ To increase the challenge, require the participants to toss the ball at least 8 feet off the ground.

⇒ Arrange all the pairs in a large circle and have one ball going from pair to pair around the room without stopping.

⇒ This activity can also be used as an "Energizer."

⇒ Form groups consisting of two pairs of participants on either side of the room. Similar to an old-fashioned egg toss, increase the distance between the pairs until only one group remains. (If outdoors, for added excitement use real eggs instead of a ball.)

| **Materials**: 1 medium-sized towel for each two participants and 1 plastic or rubber playground ball for each team. (Note: The smaller the towel, the greater the challenge.) | **Setup**: Either outdoors or a large open room | **Group Size**: 20-40 participants |

D11　House of Clay

Goal: Team Building	Ages: 6-Adult	Time: 10 minutes

Directions:

1. Divide participants into groups of 2-6 and give each group a sheet of wax paper, ball of clay, and plastic knife.
2. Explain to the groups that each will have 3 minutes to brainstorm and decide on the shape and style of a house the group is going to build. Emphasize that each participant has to contribute some part of the building.
3. Begin the brainstorming and after 3 minutes explain that each group now will have 4 minutes to sculpt the house. Give a signal to begin.
4. After 4 minutes ask each group to share their house with the entire group and explain the process which led to the house being constructed in this manner. Discuss the helpful and unhelpful aspects of the cooperation and group decision making.

Variations:

⇒　This can also be done as an individual activity.

⇒　Participants could make other objects, such as cars, machines of various types, or natural objects.

Materials: A 1' square sheet of wax paper, 3-inch ball of clay (or Play-Doh), and plastic knife per group	Setup: None	Group Size: 5-50, divided into groups of 2-6

D12　Designing a Group Picture

Goal: Team Building	Ages: 6-Adult	Time: 15 minutes

Directions:

1. Divide the participants into small groups of 4-6 and tell everyone to get in a circle.
2. One participant is given a sheet of paper to start the activity. This person has two minutes to draw on the paper. No other team member is permitted to help at this time.
3. After two minutes, another participant is to take up the project and draw for two minutes without help from other group members.
4. This continues until everyone has a turn.
5. When completed, each group should discuss their feelings about the picture and the process the members used to complete the picture.
6. Display the picture using the tape.

Variations:

⇒　At the end of each turn, have group members discuss the picture's progress for approximately one minute.

Materials: One large sheet of paper, one set of markers, and tape for each group	Setup: Hard surface to draw on	Group Size: Any size, divided into 4-6 participants per group

D13   It Takes a Little Bit of Clay

Goal: Team Building	**Ages**: 8-Adult	**Time**: 10-15 minutes

Directions:

1. Divide the participants into groups of 4-6.
2. Have each group sit in a circle and give each group a large lump of clay.
3. Put the clay in front of one group member on the wax paper, to begin the activity.
4. The leader will call out a scene or object that can be made out of clay. Some examples include: a plate of spaghetti and meatballs, a school, a produce stand, hamburger and french fries, a zoo, etc.
5. Blow the whistle to signal the groups to start. The first participant, alone, should begin designing the scene or object.
6. After 30 seconds to 1 minute, the facilitator should blow the whistle and the next participant in the circle should continue work on the sculpture. After another 30 seconds to 1 minute the leader should blow the whistle again, and so on until the leader signals a stop to the activity.
7. Each team should then share its creation with all participants and discuss the team processes that helped and hindered their performance.

Materials: A 3-inch ball of clay or Play-Doh and piece of wax paper per team and 1 whistle for the facilitator	**Setup**: A room with tables and chairs	**Group Size**: Any size, divided into groups of 4-6

D14   The Tangled Web We Weave

Goal: Team Building	**Ages**: 5-Adult	**Time**: 10-15 minutes (usually)

Directions:

1. Divide the participants into groups of 6-8.
2. Tell the participants in each group to stand in a circle, extend their left hand across the circle, and grasp the right hand of another teammate who is approximately opposite them.
3. Then have the participants extend their right hand across the circle and grasp the left hand of any other teammate.
4. Tell each group to unravel the web of interlocking arms without letting go of each other's hands.
5. The first group to finish the task wins! Have the groups discuss what was helpful and unhelpful when attempting to unravel the web.

Facilitator note: Solving this dilemma depends on participants' capacity to see the whole picture, assume a leadership role, and communicate clearly. The key lies in having participants step over each others' arms to disentangle themselves until a circle is complete. It is recommended that all participants wear casual clothing.

Materials: None	**Setup**: A large space	**Group Size**: Any size, divided into groups of 6-8

D15　Playing Your Own Tunes

| **Goal**: Team Building | **Ages**: 6-Adult | **Time**: 8-10 minutes |

Directions:

1. Organize participants into pairs.
2. Give each pair of participants a plastic bag with assorted articles (see materials).
3. Tell each pair to come up with at least two instruments to play a song on for at least 20 seconds.
4. Each pair of participants must also agree on a song to play. Allow 2 minutes of brainstorming.
5. After the brainstorming session, allow each pair 2 minutes to practice the song.
6. Each pair then performs for the whole group.

Variations:

This activity can also be used as an "Energizer."

| **Materials**: A plastic bag for every 2 participants with the following items: 4 rubber bands, 1 piece of wax paper, 1 plastic cup, 1 covered plastic container, dried beans and a comb | **Setup**: None | **Group Size**: 10-20 participants, divided into pairs |

D16　Can You Build a Pyramid?

| **Goal**: Team Building | **Ages**: 8-Adult | **Time**: 10-15 minutes |

Directions:

1. Prior to beginning the activity, cut string into three-foot pieces and tie six pieces of string to a rubber band, spacing them as evenly apart as possible. Each group will need one of these rubber bands.
2. Divide participants into groups of about six.
3. Give each group a stack of ten paper cups and one rubber band (with the strings attached).
4. Have participants put the cups upside down on a table and spread them out.
5. Challenge the group to build a pyramid out of the paper cups (4 cups on bottom, then three cups, etc.).
6. Group members may not touch cups with their hands or any other parts of their bodies.
7. Each person should hold one of the strings that are attached to the rubber band. The group should use this device to pick up the cups and place them one on top of the other.
8. Have each group process how they felt during the activity.

Variations:

⇒　Have the groups discuss their progress, make adjustments and then repeat the activity.
⇒　Rather than a pyramid, have the groups construct something else or stack the cups.

| **Materials**: For each group: 10 paper cups of the same size, 1 rubber band (must fit around the cup), 6 pieces of string (each 3' long), paper clips, scissors | **Setup**: Tables | **Group Size**: 6-50 participants, divided into groups of about 6 |

D17   Cooking Up Teamwork!

Goal: Team Building	**Ages**: 12-Adult	**Time**: 15-20 minutes

Directions:

1. Explain that when cooking a meal, if the food doesn't turn out as expected, it may be that we measured incorrectly, substituted ingredients, cooked it too long, etc.
2. In order to be a team, certain ingredients and directions are also needed.
3. Ask each group to create a recipe for "Team Success!" Distribute a "Team Success" card (see Illustration D17) to each group.
4. Instruct the groups to think of a recipe and substitute teamwork characteristics for ingredients, naming the ingredients, the quantity, the value it adds, and the time needed to "cook."
5. After 10 minutes, have each team read their recipe! (If the groups meet more than one time, keep the "Team Success" cards and have the groups make posters to remind them about good teamwork.

Variations:

⇒   Use another analogy such as roadmaps or blueprints for team building.

Materials: 1 pencil and "Team Success" card per team (see Illustration D17)	**Setup**: None	**Group Size**: 6-40, divided into groups of about 6 participants

Illustration D17: Team Success Cards for Cooking Up Teamwork

Team Success

D18   A Work of Art

Goal: Team Building | **Ages**: 12-Adult | **Time**: 15-20 minutes

Directions:

1. Divide the participants into teams of about six.
2. Have one participant gather all materials for the team.
3. Without any verbal conversation, have the team create a mural representing their group.
4. All materials should be used in some manner and each participant should contribute.
5. After everyone has contributed, the silence can be broken.
6. The team can then discuss what is missing from the picture.
7. Have each team discuss how they want to present the mural to the larger group.
8. Finally, have each team present the mural to the whole group.

Variations:

⇒ Instead of silent participation, have the group discuss what they want their mural to look like.

Materials: Finger paints (for each group), scraps of fabric and paper, markers, large sheets of paper | **Setup**: Tables and chairs | **Group Size**: Any size, divided into teams of about 6

D19   Everyone Scores

Goal: Team Building | **Ages**: 6-Adult | **Time**: 20+ minutes

Directions:

1. Divide the group into four teams and give each team a batch of stickers with the numbers on them (1, 2, 3, or 4).
2. Each participant should affix a sticker to his/her shirt with the number of their team (i.e., 1, 2, 3, or 4).
3. Teams 1 and 2 will be shooting at one large basket and teams 3 and 4 will be shooting at the other large basket.
4. Everyone should be playing at the same time.
5. The object of the game is for each participant to score a basket.
6. Play regular basketball rules, only everyone helps every player to make a basket. Every time a score is made, the person who made the basket takes off their sticker and puts it on the score board. They can't score again and must go sit on the side with their teammates and cheer.
7. The first team to successfully have everyone score is the winner. (To curb aggressiveness, any participant committing a foul must sit on the side and cannot affix their sticker to the scoreboard.)

Variations:

⇒ For smaller groups, play with two teams and when someone scores that team gets a point.

Materials: 2 basketballs, 2 large (bushel) baskets, white stickers with 1, 2, 3, or 4 written on them, poster board for a scoreboard | **Setup**: Gym area with basketball goals down | **Group Size**: 20 or more participants

D20   The Power of Paper Clips

Goal: Team Building	**Ages**: 8-Adult	**Time**: 15 minutes

Directions:

1. Sorting technique: Give a paper clip to each participant and have them divide into groups based on the color of their paper clip. (For very large groups, the leader may need a secondary sorting technique such as counting off to obtain an optimal size of 5-10 participants per group.)
2. Have each group select one person to get materials and another to act as recorder.
3. Have the groups brainstorm to determine as many uses as possible for the paper clip (5 minutes).
4. The group should then select their best idea and demonstrate that idea to the entire group (approximately 2-3 minutes of time may be necessary to prepare this demonstration).
5. Ask for a volunteer to begin the demonstrations.
6. Applaud all efforts.

Variations:

⇒   Rather than a paper clip, any common object can be substituted.

Materials: At least 1 sheet of newsprint per group; several different colored markers per group; paper clips of various colors (1 paper clip for each participant)	**Setup**: Sufficient space to divide into groups	**Group Size**: Any size

---

D21   A Pair of Yarns

Goal: Team Building	**Ages**: Teenagers and adults	**Time**: 8 minutes

Directions:

1. One participant holds all the strings at the middle with the ends protruding on either side so that no one can see which end is attached to which.
2. Each participant takes an end and in this way the group is divided into pairs who are "strung together."
3. The pairs can move to a part of the room and talk to each other for 8 minutes about any of a number of topics such as future plans for themselves, an organization, difficulties they encounter, etc.

Materials: Half as many pieces of yarn as there are participants (all the same length [about 3'] and color)	**Setup**: None	**Group Size**: 8-20 participants

D22   Advertising Our Concerns

Goal: Team Building	**Ages**: 6-Adult	**Time**: 10-15 minutes

Directions:

1. Divide participants in groups of four.
2. Give each group paper, markers, and tape.
3. Tell the groups to brainstorm and come up with a topic that everyone cares about.
4. They then need to develop a billboard which will represent their concerns.
5. After each group has finished, each billboard should be taped to the wall and discussed.

Variations:

⇒   Assign the topic according to a theme of the day (e.g., conflict resolution, team building).

Materials: Large sheets of paper, markers, tape	**Setup**: Large area	**Group Size**: Any size, divided into groups of about four

D23 So You Want to Be a Cartoonist

Goal: Team Building	**Ages**: 8-Adult	**Time**: 10 minutes

Directions:

1. Divide participants in groups of four.
2. Give each participant paper and markers.
3. Tell each group to create a comic strip on a theme of their choosing.
4. Once the decisions have been made, everyone should draw a cartoon at the same time. Tell the participants not to look at each other's drawings until finished.
5. After everyone is finished, allow time for sharing in the small groups and then with the entire group.

Variations:

⇒   Assign the theme for the groups according to a topic for the day (e.g., conflict resolution, changing families, team building).

Materials: Paper, markers	**Setup**: None	**Group Size**: Any size, divided into groups of about four

D24   Hockey Anyone?

Goal: Team Building	**Ages**: 8-Adult	**Time**: 15-20 minutes

Directions:

1. Divide the participants into groups of about six.
2. Instruct the groups that they are going to play a simple game of hockey but they have to make their own hockey sticks out of paper and tape.
3. Distribute newspaper and tape to each table. Have each participant design and make their own hockey stick.
4. After all hockey sticks are made, it is time to play hockey! Each group should try to hit the ball with their hockey sticks into the other goal.
5. Let the game begin! Play until it is time to change to a new activity.

Materials: Masking tape, news-print, plastic balls, 2 goals (4 chairs or cones)	**Setup**: Room with tables, then a large open field or room	**Group Size**: 12 or more

D25   Alphabet Scavenger Hunt

Goal: Team Building	**Ages**: 8-Adult	**Time**: 20 minutes

Directions:

1. Divide the participants into several groups.
2. Tell participants that each group is to fill up the bag with 26 items; each item's name must begin with a different letter of the alphabet. If the item cannot be removed or placed in the bag, an index card should be used to name the item
3. The group with the most items wins.
4. As a large group, ask several participants in each group to select one item from the bag that represents themselves as a person and share it with the group.

Variations:

⇒ Each team can pick an item from their bag which best describes how they work as a team.

Materials: A bag for each team, index cards, markers	**Setup**: More than one room with lots of "stuff" in it	**Group Size**: Any size, divided into 2 or more grouops

D26   It's a Banner Session!

Goal: Team Building	**Ages**: 5-Adult	**Time**: 5-10 minutes

Directions:

1. Give each participant a banner.
2. Ask the participants to review in their mind the ways teamwork has been shown during this session.
3. Instruct participants to draw symbols that represent this session for them.
4. Ask participants to share their banners with the person next to them (or the entire group).

Variations:

⇒   Organize the participants in groups and have the group make a banner and share their banner with other groups.

Materials: Pre-cut paper banners (one for each person) with the word "Teamwork" in the center of 11" x 17" sheets of paper, scissors, markers	**Setup**: Large room for groups	**Group Size**: Any size

D27   Banner Display

Goal: Team Building	**Ages**: 8-Adult	**Time**: 20 minutes

Directions:

1. Explain to the participants that symbols are all around us and help us to create understanding.
2. Divide the participants in groups of about 6.
3. Distribute materials and have each group create a banner using symbols that represent the group as a total group and as individuals.
4. When completed, ask participants to put the banners on the wall and share the meaning of the banners with the entire group.

Materials: Roll of butcher paper, colored markers, tape	**Setup**: None	**Group Size**: Any size, divided into groups of about 6

D28   What's in a Name?

Goal: Team Building	**Ages**: 12-Adult	**Time**: 5-10 minutes

Directions:

1. Give each participant a team name card and ask them to find the other members of their group by searching for participants with identical cards.
2. Have each group sit at a table together.
3. Ask each group to think about their team name, describe desirable team characteristics, and design a logo for the group.
4. Ask each group to share their results with the other teams.

Variations:

⇒ At the end of the session, ask the teams to create a new name that describes the group even better.

Materials: Team name cards (see Illustration D28)	**Setup**: Tables and chairs	**Group Size**: 10-50 divided into groups of about 5

Illustration D28: What's In A Name?

Woodchucks	Rabbits	Arabian Horses	Camels	Grasshoppers
Panthers	Otters	Leopards	Dolphins	Eagles

D29　　　　I'm in the Money

| Goal: Team Building | Ages: 8-Adult | Time: Any amount of time |

Directions:

1. Before participants arrive, put $1,000 [or any amount] in various denominations of play money in half of the envelopes and write "To Give" on each envelope.
2. Write "Recognition" on the other envelopes.
3. As participants arrive, tape one of each type of envelope to them.
4. Instruct participants to use all the money in the "To Give" envelopes to reward one another for contributing insights or ideas. The different denominations are to help place value on the contributions.
5. By the end of the session, they are to spend all their recognition dollars.

Variations:

⇒ Use poker chips instead of play money with different amounts on them.
⇒ At the end of the session, allow participants to spend the play money on prizes or treats.

| Materials: Play money ($1,000 per participant), two envelopes per participant, prizes with different values (optional) | Setup: None | Group Size: Any size |

D30　　　Building in the Dark

| Goal: Team Building | Ages: 5-Adult | Time: 10-15 minutes |

Directions:

1. Divide the participants into groups of six or more.
2. Blindfold half of the group.
3. Have the other half build some sort of structure with about 10 blocks.
4. Ask one person in the group to draw the structure.
5. The blindfolded group must then build the structure with instructions from the sighted group.
6. The sighted group must not touch any of the pieces or the participants when giving instructions.
7. After the structure is built, have the group take off their blindfolds and see how close they came to making the structure.
8. Switch roles and repeat steps 2-7.
9. Discussion for the group:
    ⇒ Which role was harder for you? Why?
    ⇒ Were you frustrated at any time?
    ⇒ What solutions did you come up with to complete this task?
    ⇒ How is this activity like real life?

| Materials: Numerous wooden blocks, 2' cloth for blindfolds (1 per participant, cloths should not be re-used during this session), paper, pencils | Setup: Large area | Group Size: 12 or more, divided into groups of 6 or more |

D31   Don't Knock the Pin Over

Goal: Team Building	**Ages**: 5-Adult	**Time**: 8-10 minutes

Directions:

1. Mark off an area of about 40' by 40' using the orange cones. The number of areas is determined by the participants. Set the bowling pin in the center.
2. Break the participants into groups of about 10. Give each group the same number of balls.
3. Tell each team they are to hit the bowling pin with one of the balls without knocking it over.
4. At no time can anyone get into the marked area.
5. Each team will try to be the first to hit the bowling pin with a ball and may try to keep the others from touching the pin with a ball by knocking any ball out of the area.
6. Rules of play:
⇒   Anyone can roll a ball at any time.
⇒   The balls may be used to bump other balls.
⇒   Once a ball is in the area, it can't be retrieved but can be bumped out.
⇒   If the pin is knocked over, the whole group must start over.
⇒   The first team to hit the pin gets 5 points, and any other team to touch the pin gets 2 points.
⇒   Keep playing until all balls are in the middle.
7. Discuss the strategies used and how teams could improve performance.

Materials: For each group: One bowling pin (or a plastic 2-liter jug filled one-third with water), as many different kinds of balls as you can gather (rubber balls, fuzzy soft balls, foam balls), four orange cones or other markers	**Setup**: Each group requires a large open space (about 40' x 40')	**Group Size**: Any size, divided into groups of about 10

D32   I Can Help!

Goal: Team Building	**Ages**: 8-Adult	**Time**: 15 minutes

Directions:

1. Divide the participants into groups of 3 or 4.
2. Instruct each group to create a first aid kit using the items given them.
3. Each group must decide and describe how each item will be used.
4. One member of the group will then present their first aid kits to the entire group.

Variations:

⇒   Change the goal to developing an "emotional" first aid kit (i.e., to cheer someone up who is emotionally hurt).

Materials: For each group: 2 paper cups, 2 rulers, 6 rubber bands, 6 paper clips, 3 pieces of colored paper, 6 poker chips, 15 mailing labels, 4 pieces of string (each 4 feet long), 1 envelope, 2 pencils (unsharpened).	**Setup**: Tables or desks	**Group Size**: Any size, divided into groups of 3 or 4

D33   Swat the Balloon Relay

Goal: Team Building	**Ages**: 5-Adult	**Time**: 10-15 minutes

Directions:

1. Have participants in each group (of no more than 10) line up in two rows and face the person in the other row (see Illustration D33).
2. The object is to keep the balloon in the air going up and down the rows.
3. Give the two flyswatters to the first participants in each row (participants 1 & 2).
4. After participant #1 swats the balloon to participant #2, he hands the flyswatter to participant #3, participant #2 swats the balloon to participant #3 then hands the flyswatter to participant #4, and so on until the balloon makes it all the way up the line and back again. In the Illustration (D33), the balloon travels in the order 1-2-3-4-5-6-7-8-9-10-9-8-7-6-5-4-3-2-1. The first flyswatter travels in the order 1-3-5-7-9-7-5-3-1, and the 2nd flyswatter travels in the order 2-4-6-8-10-8-6-4-2).
5. If a person lets the balloon drop, the group must begin over. The first team that goes back and forth five times wins.

Materials: Two flyswatters per group, several inflated balloons	**Setup**: Open area	**Group Size**: Any size, divided into groups of about 10

Illustration D33: Swat the Balloon Relay

D34   You're a Mummy

| **Goal**: Team Building | **Ages**: 5-Adult | **Time**: 15 minutes |

Directions:

1. Divide participants into groups of 3-4.
3. Designate one member of the group to be the mummy.
3. The other team members are given 5 minutes to "wrap" the mummy from head to toe. There should be some leg movement allowed, so the mummy can walk.
4. At the end of five minutes, the mummies should be escorted about the room by group members.
5. As an entire group, discuss the following questions:
⇒   What times caused anxiety?
⇒   How does it feel to be confined and have to rely on others?
⇒   How careful were group members?

| **Materials**: Several rolls of toilet paper, masking tape | **Setup**: Large area | **Group Size**: Any size, divided into groups of 3-4 |

D35   A Positive Five Minutes

| **Goal**: Team Building | **Ages**: 5-Adult | **Time**: 5 minutes |

Directions:

1. Prior to the beginning of the session, write the numbers 1-10 on strips of paper (one number per strip) and put them in each group's bag.
2. Divide the participants into groups of 8-10.
3. Ask the group to sit in a circle.
4. Have each person remove a slip of paper from the bag. The person with the lowest number starts the game.
5. The person who starts the game has to say something positive or uplifting. Announce the activity will last for 5 minutes and begin timing.
6. In numerical order, have each participant state a compliment until the five minutes are up.

Variations:

⇒   If a competition is desired, eliminate members who repeat a used compliment, or who cannot come up with a compliment or positive statement in less than 15 seconds.

| **Materials**: A watch or clock, and one paper bag for each group with slips of paper numbered 1-10 | **Setup**: Large area | **Group Size**: 8-25, divided into groups of 8-10 |

D36　　Double Circles

Goal: Team Building　　**Ages**: 6-Adult　　**Time**: 10-15 minutes

Directions:

1. Divide participants into pairs. If the number in the group is uneven, the person without a partner becomes the referee; if even, the facilitator becomes the referee.
2. Two circles should then be formed, one inside the other. One partner is to be in the inside circle and one in the outside circle.
3. In a manner similar to musical chairs, when the music starts, the participants in the inside circle are to move clockwise, and the participants in the outer circle are to move counterclockwise. When the music stops the partners are to go to one another, touch shoulders and squat down. The last partners to locate each other and squat down are out of the game and will referee the next round.
4. The game continues until one pair remains.

Materials: CD player, CDs　　**Setup**: Large room　　**Group Size**: 12 or more, divided into pairs

D37　　I Can Use It

Goal: Team Building　　**Ages**: 5-Adult　　**Time**: 10 minutes

Directions:

1. Before beginning, select an item that is readily available, such as a rubber band, pencil, button, toothpick, etc., and place one object inside each paper bag. Each group should receive the same object in the paper bag.
2. Explain that this is a contest. Each group will have five minutes to brainstorm as many uses as possible for the object inside the paper bag.
3. Each group should identify a recorder to write down suggestions. Give each group a pen and piece of paper. For groups of very young children, have an older child or adult act as recorder.
4. Hand each group a paper bag and tell them to begin.
5. Stop the brainstorming after five minutes.
6. Have each recorder read the list. As a whole, discuss what did and did not facilitate good team performance.

Variations:

⇒　Participants can form a single circle and each person in turn can state a use for the object. No repeat uses are allowed.
⇒　After the first round, allow participants to discuss and share methods that facilitated brainstorming and then conduct a second round with a different object.
⇒　This activity can also be used for "Energizer."

Materials: For each team, provide a paper bag with a small item inside (e.g., rubber band, pencil, button, toothpick, etc.), pen, paper　　**Setup**: None　　**Group Size**: Any size, divided into groups of 4-6

D38   Walk That Walk!

Goal: Team Building	**Ages**: 7-Adult	**Time**: 10-15 minutes

Directions:

1. Ask participant pairs to stand side by side.
2. Give each pair long strips of cloth or masking tape and ask them to tie or tape themselves at the ankle. Have the pairs take a few steps forward.
3. Next have two pairs join together so a foursome is now joined and walking forward.
4. Continue this joining until lines of participants the width of the room are joined together and walking together.

Materials: 2' strips of cloth, masking tape	**Setup**: None	**Group Size**: Any size, divided into pairs

---

D39   Stand Up and Cheer!

Goal: Team Building	**Ages**: 7-Adult	**Time**: 5-10 minutes

Directions:

1. Ask participants to divide into teams of three to four.
2. Ask participants to sit down as a group with their backs and shoulders to each other, link elbows, and then stand up without unlinking arms.
3. Cheer after the team finishes the task.
4. Ask each group to find another group and repeat the procedure as two groups combined.
5. This should continue until people are joining together as an entire group.
6. Lead a loud group cheer for a job well done.

Materials: None	**Setup**: Open space	**Group Size**: 3 or more, divided into groups of 3-4

D40 Building a Bridge of Strength

Goal: Team Building

Ages: 8-Adult

Time: 10-15 minutes

Directions:
1. Divide the participants into groups of about 10.
2. Give each group plates and markers. (Number of plates varies by size of room.)
3. Ask each participant to take a paper plate and write down one of their own strengths on it. Each should do more than one plate.
4. After the group has finished writing down their strengths, they need to make a bridge from one side of the room to the other by taping the plates together, but must stand on the plates during construction.
5. When building the bridge, only plates marked with strengths can be used.
6. At no time may anyone's feet touch the floor.
7. If more plates are needed by any group, they have to write down more strengths.

Materials: Many paper plates, markers, tape

Setup: Large area

Group Size: 10 or more, divided into groups of about 10

D41   Throw Out the Lifeline!

Goal: Team Building

Ages: 8-Adult

Time: 10-15 minutes

Directions:
1. Create an area in the room or outside that is a "fast-moving river." The river should be about 20-30 feet across.
2. Divide the participants into groups of about 8. Have them select one member to go across the river. Tell the group they are on a rescue mission and they must create a lifeline to rescue their friend. (They can use shoelaces, clothing, tree branches, or other materials found in the environment.)
3. The group must use anything they can find to make a lifeline for the stranded group member. The lifeline must reach all the way to the other side when thrown. If it goes in the river, it must be reeled in and thrown again.
4. Once the lifeline reaches the other side, the stranded participant may be pulled to safety.
5. Have the entire group discuss the following:
⇒ What did the various participants do to help facilitate the task?
⇒ Would you want to be across a real river and have to depend on your group to rescue you? Why or why not?

Materials: None

Setup: None

Group Size: Any size, divided into groups of about 8

D42   How Many Can I List?

Goal: Team Building	**Ages**: 8-Adult	**Time**: 5-6 minutes

Directions:

1. Divide participants into groups of about four to six.
2. Explain there will be a short competition to stimulate thinking.
3. Distribute one resource sheet, "How Many Can I List?" (see Illustration D42) to each participant.
4. Tell participants they will have three minutes to think about answers they would like to give. They may jot down answers on the sheet if they like.
5. Have each group select a recorder and one topic the group would like to attempt. (If possible, be sure all the topics are covered.)
6. Let the groups make a master list of one of the topics. They have three minutes for this activity. The recorder should list the items on the newsprint with markers. The group with the most answers wins.

Materials: One handout (see Illustration D42) per participant, pens/pencils, newsprint, markers	**Setup**: None	**Group Size**: 4-50, divided into groups of about 4-6

Illustration D42: How Many Can I List?

1. Things you are most likely to laugh at.

2. Places you are most likely to go on the weekend.

3. Places you are most likely to go to on weekdays.

4. Things that make you angry.

5. Things that make you cry.

D43   Tied to Work

| **Goal**: Team Building | **Ages**: 5-Adult | **Time**: 15 minutes |

Directions:

1. Divide participants into groups of four.
2. Ask the group members to stand in a circle facing each other and to hold out their arms.
3. Tie each group together so that each person is tied to both neighbors' wrists.
4. Now that the group is "tied to work" give them a task to do together. Each person must contribute.
5. Tasks may include: Create a mural; wrap packages; pour a cup of water for each group participant; make a peanut butter sandwich; or any other fun activity you can think of.

Caution: All cloth strips should not be used again until washed.

| **Materials**: Cloth strips and other items depending on the activity selected | **Setup**: Large open space | **Group Size**: Any size, divided into groups of 4 |

D44   We Can Blow Bubbles

| **Goal**: Team Building | **Ages**: 5-Adult | **Time**: 10 minutes |

Directions:

1. Divide the participants into groups of about 4.
2. Give the group all of their supplies and explain their task is to make bubbles (that float in the air) out of what has been given to them. Challenge groups to make the biggest bubble!

Hint: Soap and water can be mixed together to make a solution. The yarn or string may be used to make a bubble by putting the yarn/string through two straws and tying it into a loop so that it makes a square. Hold the straws and dip it into the bubble mix and try to make a bubble. You may want to cut the straws in half to make smaller bubble makers or simply use your fingers to make a circle that will create a bubble.

| **Materials**: Bowl, liquid soap, water, drinking straws, yarn/string, towels, scissors | **Setup**: Outdoors | **Group Size**: Any size, divided into groups of about 4 |

D45   Can We Do It?

| **Goal**: Team Building | **Ages**: 5-Adult | **Time**: 10-15 minutes |

Directions:

Note: Before the activity starts, areas should be marked off. The area should be large enough that everyone can fit in it, but small enough that not everyone's feet can easily stand in the area.

1. Divide the participants into groups of 15-20.
2. Show the participants the marked off areas.
3. Challenge the participants to fit everyone onto the area without anyone touching the outside area or falling off. Groups must stay in for at least ten seconds.
4. At the end of each activity, have the groups report to the whole group any strategies or challenges each encountered.

| **Materials**: Masking tape | **Setup**: Open space | **Group Size**: 15-100, divided into groups of 15-20 |

D46   Banding Together!

| **Goal**: Team Building | **Ages**: 5-Adult | **Time**: 5 minutes |

Directions:

1. Divide participants into groups of about 6-8.
2. The leader should take one large elastic band to each group and put the band over the wrist of one person in the group.
3. Have everyone hold hands in a circle.
4. Have each group pass the band from one to another without releasing hands until the band has gone around the whole group.
5. Share strategies and then try again.

Variations:

⇒   Use this as a group competition with prizes!

| **Materials**: Large elastic band (2 yards in length and sewn to form a circle) | **Setup**: Large open space | **Group Size**: Any size, divided into groups of about 6-8 |

D47　　Banding Together 2

| **Goal**: Team Building | **Ages**: 5-Adult | **Time**: 10 minutes |

Directions:

1. Divide the participants into groups of four.
2. Instruct the group to place one elastic band around the waists of all participants in the group simultaneously.
3. The group needs to discuss what kind of group movements they will make when the music comes on. They can select hand, foot, or body movements.
4. Share strategies and then try again.

| **Materials**: Tape player/CD player, tape/CD of different kinds of music that are easy to move to, large elastic band (2 yards in length, sewn together in a circle) for each group | **Setup**: Large area | **Group Size**: Any size, divided into groups of about 4 |

D48　　Banding Together 3

| **Goal**: Team Building | **Ages**: 5-Adult | **Time**: 5 minutes |

Directions:

1. Divide participants into groups of about 6-8.
2. Give one elastic band to each group and have participants put the band around their waists simultaneously.
3. The members of each group are to put their arms around the waists of the people on each side of them.
4. Without touching the band with hands or arms, the band is then to be moved to the group's shoulders and then back to their waists. Move the band then to the ankles, then up to their waists again!
5. Share strategies and then try again.

| **Materials**: One large elastic band per group (2 yards in length, sewn to form a circle) | **Setup**: Large area | **Group Size**: Any size, divided into groups of about 6-8 |

D49   Poetry in Motion

| **Goal**: Team Building | **Ages**: 8-Adult | **Time**: 10-15 minutes |

Directions:

1. Divide the participants into groups of about 6.
2. Pile the materials in the center of each table.
3. The challenge for each group is to take the materials and try to make a machine that is in motion and, once in motion, will set other things in motion without any intervention. (An example might be the marble rolls and hits the spoon, which tips the cup, which dumps the sand, etc.
4. Have each team share their machines with each other.

| **Materials**: For each table: marbles, cups, paper towel tubes, toilet paper tubes, balls, string, small wooden sticks, plastic spoons, paper clips, pencil, fabric scraps, sand, buckets, tin foil, moving car (toy), plastic wrap | **Setup**: Tables | **Group Size**: Any size, divided into groups of about 6 |

D50 I Can Make a Square Blindfolded

| **Goal**: Team Building | **Ages**: 8-Adult | **Time**: 10 minutes |

Directions:

1. Divide participants into groups of 4, have the teammates face each other, and make sure the groups are spaced around the room so no one will bump into another participant.
2. Tell the participants to blindfold each other.
3. Place a rope loop at the feet of each team.
4. Ask each team to pick up the rope and form a perfect square with their rope without peeking. Each participant should hold the rope with only 1 finger/hand.
5. Once the group believes it has created a perfect square, the leader should measure it with a tape measure, announce the dimensions, and allow the team to either try again or take off their blindfolds to see the result.
6. As a group, discuss strategies for improving performance, communication, and teamwork.

Variations:

⇒ After the discussion on improving performance, have the groups try again.
⇒ Have the teams make other shapes and letters.
⇒ This activity can also be used as an Energizer or Starter.

| **Materials**: One tape measure, a long piece (at least 15 feet long) of string or rope for each team (tied together to form a loop). One piece of cloth (at least 30 inches long) for each participant to use as a blindfold. (Do not reuse the blindfolds!) | **Setup**: None | **Group Size**: Any size, divided into groups of 4 |

D51 General Motors, Here I Come

| **Goal**: Team Building | **Ages**: 10-Adult | **Time**: 15-20 minutes |

Directions:
1. Tell participants they are all going to design a new type of car.
2. Tell participants to divide into groups of 6 or more (must be an even number, but no more than 10 to a group).
3. Divide each group into 2 subgroups. Instruct one subgroup to design the front end of the car and the other subgroup to design the rear end of the car.
4. Give each group a large sheet of paper and markers. Allow 5 minutes for participants to draw their part of the van.
5. After 5 minutes, have the 2 subgroups brainstorm together to develop a sales presentation promoting the qualities of the new car.
6. Have the group develop and present a humorous "commercial" to be presented to the entire group.
7. The group will select a salesperson for the car to give a 1 minute (or less) sales pitch to the entire group.

Variations:
⇒ As an alternative, the groups can design a house, clothing article, etc.

| **Materials**: Large sheets of paper, markers | **Setup**: Areas for groups to work | **Group Size**: 6-20, must be an even number |

D52 Spell It Out for Me!

| **Goal**: Team Building | **Ages**: 12-Adult | **Time**: 7-10 minutes |

Directions:
1. Organize participants into groups of 6-20.
2. As practice, play the song *YMCA* and have the participants spell out *YMCA* with the song.
3. Instruct each group to come up with a name or phrase that has meaning to the group (usually related to the group topic).
4. Each group will spell and act out their word (acronym) or phrase.
5. Give the groups 5-7 minutes to prepare and practice a skit, song or rap amongst themselves.
6. Ask each group to spell out their word or acronym by performing for the entire group.

Variations:
⇒ The groups could spell out a closure message such as "WE ARE ALL _____" (name of organization, school, etc.)

| **Materials**: Tape or CD of YMCA song (by the Village People), tape-recorder or CD player, cards to write names on. | **Setup**: Large open space | **Group Size**: 15 or more participants |

D53 I've Never Seen That Animal Before

| **Goal**: Team Building | **Ages**: 6-Adult | **Time**: 15 minutes |

Directions:

1. Divide participants into groups of about four.
2. Tell the groups to develop a new species of animal and the environment each would live in using the materials given.
3. After about 10 minutes, have each group present their new species to the entire group.
4. Discuss the positives and negatives of some of the species living in the same environment. Also, discuss what the animal species may represent (e.g., values, character traits, beliefs.).

| **Materials**: Paper, markers, tape, pencils, crayons | **Setup**: Tables or desks | **Group Size**: Any size, divided into groups of about 4 |

Section E

Closure

E 1   The Gifts We Bring

Goal: Closure

Ages: 8-Adult

Time: 10-15 minutes

Directions:

1. Before the session begins, purchase some candy. Wrap the candy in many layers and make sure you use lots of tape.
2. Gather the group in a circle with everyone sitting down on the floor. Start playing music and give the gift to the participant to your right. The gift continues to be passed around from one participant to the next until the music stops. In the tradition of musical chairs, the person who has the gift when the music stops unwraps a single layer of paper and shares one thing learned in the session.
3. Start the music again and repeat the procedure. The participant who ultimately unwraps the present should share the contents with everyone.

Variations:

⇒   Use more than one gift if you have a large group.

Materials: Music source, bag of candy, tape, newsprint & wrapping paper

Setup: Large area

Group Size: Any size

E 2   It's Time to Say Goodbye

Goal: Closure

Ages: 5-Adult

Time: 10-15 minutes

Directions:

1. Tell the participants it is time to say good-bye.
2. Form a large circle and count off by two's.
3. Tell the 1's to take two steps in so an inner circle will be formed.
4. Participants in circle one should turn and face someone in circle two and say their good-byes in a way that they find comfortable.
5. Circle two should rotate one person to the right and repeat the process until everyone has said good-bye.

Materials: None

Setup: None

Group Size: Any size

E 3   Circle Summary

Goal: Closure   **Ages**: 6-Adult   **Time**: 8-10 minutes

Directions:

1. Ask participants to form a circle.
2. Have participants close their eyes and think of 3 things each enjoyed or got out of the session.
3. Give the passing object to a participant and have him/her state one thing he/she thought of.
4. Have the participant pass the object to the next participant and have that participant share one thing.
5. Continue around the group in this fashion until each participant has had a turn.

Variations:

⇒ Participants can also share how they would like to change the session, where each would like to go from this point, or another topic of importance to the group.

Materials: A ball, bean bag, or some other object that can be passed

Setup: Large, open area

Group Size: Any size

E 4   Let's Stay in Touch

Goal: Closure   **Ages**: 10-Adult   **Time**: 10-15 minutes

Directions:

1. Prior to the closing half hour of a session, post newsprint on the walls around the room.
2. Instruct participants to write their name, address, phone numbers, and e-mail address on the newsprint during a break.
3. Allow participants time to copy the names and contact information they may want for future reference.

Materials: Newsprint, masking tape, paper, and markers

Setup: None

Group Size: Any size

E 5   Once Upon A Time

Goal: Closure	**Ages**: 5-Adult	**Time**: 5-10 minutes

All of us love to listen to a great story or have enjoyed various fairy tales. This is your group's chance to enjoy making one.

Directions:

1. Ask the participants to sit in a circle.
2. Explain that "Today we are going to create a story about _____." (Your topic will depend on what your session is about.)
3. Begin the story with "Once upon a time…" Explain that each participant in the circle must add 3-5 sentences to the story. Go around the circle as many time as is necessary to complete the story.

Variations:

⇒   Have one person record the story so it can be read back.
⇒   Tape record or videotape the performance and play it back to participants.

Materials: None	**Setup**: None	**Group Size**: 5 or more participants

---

E 6   I Think I Can!

Goal: Closure	**Ages**: 6-Adult	**Time**: 4-5 minutes

Directions:

1. Ask participants to pair up.
2. Tell participants to think of one idea they could use from the session during the next week (meeting, day, etc.)
3. Have each participant share the idea with a partner.
4. Ask the partners to shake hands and say "I think I can! I think I can!"
5. Have each participant wish their partner good luck in trying out the ideas.

Materials: None	**Setup**: None	**Group Size**: Any size, divided into pairs

100

E 7   Tools of the Trade

Goal: Closure

Ages: 14-Adult

Time: 5-10 minutes

Directions:

1. Give each participant a tool card (cut out from Illustration E7) as he/she comes into the room.
2. Participants can be grouped by their "tool" cards for session activities, if desired.
3. At the end of the session, relate the following story to the group:

   A man bought an electric saw from a local store. After several hours he came back and said it didn't cut the wood right. The manager took it to the back area of the store, plugged it in, and found nothing wrong with it. The man went home, tried it again, and came back with the same complaint. The manager said "Come in the back with me and we'll try it together." As the manager plugged it in, the man said, "What is that noise?" The moral is that a tool is no good unless you know how to use it.

4. Pass out one "Tools of the Trade" worksheet to each participant.
5. Have the participants gather in groups based on their tool cards and ask participants to use the "Tools of the Trade" sheet to draw analogies between the tools on the sheet and the tools they learned during this session.
6. Tell participants to add other tools they felt they had used or learned about during the session.
7. Have each smaller group share their tools with the entire group.

Materials: One "Tools of the Trade" sheet (see Illustration E7), and "Tool" cards (for grouping) per participant

Setup: None

Group Size: 4-25 participants

Illustration: E7: Tools of the Trade

Directions: Use the tools to draw analogies between the tools on the sheet and the ones you have learned during the session.

Tools Learned During the Session

Tools

Hammer

Nail

Dustpan & Brush

Tape measurer

Wrench

E 8   "Let's Get Poppin'"

| **Goal**: Closure | **Ages**: 8-Adult | **Time**: 10 minutes |

Directions:

1. Use this activity for brainstorming new ideas to solve a problem or dilemma.
2. As a group, decorate the grocery bag to look like a popcorn bag and fill it with popcorn cutouts (see Illustration E8).
3. Near the end of each session, have each participant pick a kernel of popcorn from the bag.
4. Encourage participants to think of an idea that would help their group or team to "get poppin'"!
5. Have the participants put their ideas on the paper popcorn.
6. When finished, have each participant share their "poppin' good ideas" with the group and place their popcorn kernel in the bag.

Variations:

⇒ Put bowls of real popcorn on each table for participants to enjoy.

| **Materials**: Markers, white paper, scissors, 1 large paper grocery bag, numerous popcorn cutouts (see Illustration E8) | **Setup**: Tables and chairs | **Group Size**: 10-50 participants |

Illustration E8: Let's Get Poppin'!

E9   The Enjoyment Marquee

| **Goal**: Closure | **Ages**: 8-Adult | **Time**: 5 minutes |

Directions:

1. Tape the large paper or poster on the wall.
2. Distribute one sticky note to each participant.
3. Ask each participant to write one thing he or she enjoyed about the session.
4. Have participants place their sticky notes on the poster and spend a few minutes reading what others have written.

| **Materials**: Large poster or paper, markers, crayons, tape, enough sticky notes for each participant | **Setup**: None | **Group Size**: Any size |

E10   For Your Scrapbook

| **Goal**: Closure | **Ages**: 8-Adult | **Time**: 10-15 minutes |

Directions:

1. Divide the participants into groups of about 4.
2. Tell the groups to come up with 4 living snapshots of any event that has taken place during the session or over several sessions. (A snapshot should consist of a group posed in a certain way. Everyone should be included.)
3. Groups should choose a narrator and display their snapshots. (Optional: A camera can be used to snap the pictures.)
4. Applaud all snapshots.
5. Have participants share things each will remember.

| **Materials**: Camera (optional) | **Setup**: None | **Group Size**: 4-50 divided into groups of about 4 |

E 11   Brick by Brick

Goal: Closure	**Ages**: 8-Adult	**Time**: 20 minutes

Directions:

1. Distribute pencils and about 20 paper bricks to each group.
2. Have the participants write things learned during the day (entire experience) on the bricks.
3. Tell the groups to build a creative structure using the paper bricks and tape.
4. Have participants share what they learned with the group and what the structure symbolizes.

Materials: Paper bricks (see Illustration E11), pencils, markers, tape, scissors	**Setup**: None	**Group Size**: Any size, divided into groups of about 4

Illustration E11: Brick by Brick

Cut the shape along the solid line, fold along the dotted lines, and tape the edges to form a brick.

E12 "Egg"zactly How DO We Look?

Goal: Closure	**Ages**: 5-Adult	**Time**: 10-15 minutes

Directions:

1. Distribute an egg and a marker to each person.
2. Tell participants to decorate the egg to look like themselves.
3. When everyone has finished, put the eggs in the cartons. Mix up the cartons. Have participants select an egg that is not theirs.
4. Ask the participant to decide who the egg belongs to and give the egg back to the owner.
5. Have each member crack their egg into the large bowl.
6. Discuss how the eggs were the same and different on the outside and the inside and ways we are all the same and different on the inside and outside.

Materials: Eggs, markers, large bowl, egg cartons	**Setup**: Desks or tables	**Group Size**: Any size